Why I Want to Die

(a poetic dialogue of divorce and recovery)

By B.L. Phipps

Copyright © 2005 by B.L. Phipps

ISBN 0-7414-2659-5

Published by:

INFI∞ITY
PUBLISHING.COM

1094 New DeHaven Street, Suite 100
West Conshohocken, PA 19428-2713
Info@buybooksontheweb.com
www.buybooksontheweb.com
Toll-free (877) BUY BOOK
Local Phone (610) 941-9999
Fax (610) 941-9959

Printed in the United States of America

Printed on Recycled Paper

Published August 2005

Introduction

Thank you for coming.

The following poem started in July 1999. As I explored my feelings, it was obvious I was depressed. I talked to a therapist, but the feelings persisted. I had decided to see what I could do to write a response to this person in the poem during this time. In turn though, I found, that the response often was not enough. The "patient" would return a response to the "therapist." This went on through October of 2003. It still goes on, as I explore the feelings I have. These feelings were intense as I had (still have) these feelings brought on by a marriage, which tragically was ending in divorce. Announced to me by my wife, she was divorcing me in September of 2002, finalized in the fall of 2003. This poem covers my problems and feelings that come with the claim of being Christian and having this become a part of one's life. If you are depressed, get help.

Divorce is something that goes against my being. I had no choice in the matter. What is my response? The mechanisms that I used to examine the feelings still exist. I will have to use them again until God, in His mercy, shall grant a better solution than the one I have proposed for my "patient." (God was merciful.) For many, this is their plight, and many do not take the advice given to this "patient." Those who do are leading a better life because of it. This, then, is the exploring of my feelings – feelings that I still battle with from time to time. It is depressing, but it is still life as I was experiencing it. This could also be perhaps (more so?) between a preacher and a member of the congregation. But whichever it is, it is a struggle that is very painful to discuss my life and work through to an end that is finally a healing one. Hopefully, this will result in a happy life for both the one going through these struggles and those close to them.

As one reads the poem, there are recurring themes. Due to the nature of this state of mind, it is not like a math problem when one has the answer, then one simply uses it to move on. Many times, even after an answer is grasped as being correct, help is needed to apply the answer as the state of mind persists. As physical therapy is used to strengthen physical muscles, mental therapy is used to strengthen states of mind. The difference is that with these muscles, they have the ability to resist or help more with their therapy than muscles which have no will of their own. The pain returns, and returns, so feelings again have to be dealt with in a compassionate way. Also, as with other medical problems, there is sometimes more than one solution; if one solution does not work, another will be used. The patient will usually bring back what the "results" were, and another perspective will be used to try again from another angle and see if that works.

Assuming the person is indeed interested in healing and to the degree they are interested in being helped out of their mental state and helped with their "problem," their progress will be made accordingly. If a person is only mediocre about recovery, then so will be the results. Thus it is with this patient; the same "problems" persist. But the therapist tries to talk to the patient and encourages a view from another perspective, or a reminder that this idea or concept does work if it is indeed used. This is a simplified explanation. I have had a lot of thought, and this work spans several years. Sometimes an answer or response would not come for several weeks.

Five other books I have found helpful are:

Ecclesiastes and parts of Paul's letters in the *New Testament*
Feeling Good .... By David D. Burns M.D.
Six Pillars of Self-Esteem .... By Nathaniel Branden
The Seven Habits of Highly Effective People .... By Steven Covey
Marriage & Divorce .... By John L. Edwards

Thank you for your time,

B.L. Phipps

To my friends and family who have supported me, thank you.

Table of Contents

Why I Want to Die

By B. L. Phipps

The words of the therapist will be in bold type.
The words of the patient will be in italics.

Session One

The therapist asked, "Why?"
Why do you want to die?
Is there some mystery you cannot solve?
Or feeling or reason or emotion you cannot absolve?

The reason, kind Sir, I can speak
For this world, I guess, I am too meek
As to the reason I want to die
I shall surely tell you the reason why

My life is over and so I desire
To commit my body to the fire
God is silent to my prayer
I feel as though I am speaking to the air

There are no comforting arms to hold me tight
No loving voice to say so in the night
No welcome to my call
Or entrance at my answer to her call

This would not be so bad says I
But the Bible denies all others until I die
Condemned to live alone with her, or without
When we speak our differences we too easily shout

To speak or be silent I know the loss
She lives and behaves as though she is boss
I earn too little for her buying
I am too easily content with my low pay she's crying

So a cold shoulder I do earn
No, affection, so I burn!
Even flowers and a hug
I'll be asked what do you want, and there's a bug

1

Bury the feelings into a pit
The feelings only crawl out of it
Deeper feelings into the bowels of my being
They only creep out and send me reeling

Think and reason, I can do, but empty, I am impaired
The more I search, no options, none, I am despaired
To deny the loneliness I cannot cure
The ever-tightening emotional noose knot I have to endure

I have balanced my hopes and dreams
Against the loveless stress, it is heavier it seems
To end my life, others benefit the more
Donate my organs, and thoughts for others to explore

How cold it is and none to warm
There is no heat for me in any form
In a sense, I am dead
My life is as valueless as lead

There is no virtue in the living
So I will die in my last giving
That is the reason I want to die
Selfish? Perhaps, but I've said no lie

My energies cannot fight these things
They all the more closely to me cling
I wish to end my life
For the benefit of others and end my strife

That is why, Sir, why
I want to die

You say you want to die
The weight is crushing you, you cry
I would propose a possible solution
A way of seeing a peaceful resolution

Understand the pain you suffer and the words you utter
Our compound sins create the gold and the gutter
To be self-righteous is the worst kind of blindness
Looking down or looking up, it is still shortsightedness

Be aware you have a soul for heaven, and its Maker
To live less than its value insults its Creator
To see our choices for good or evil, we knowing little of our life
Did I, we, decide right and wrong, our soul's reflections of strife

You are right, to live without Love is a great pain
To find it faithful and true a great gain
The pain isn't illusion, neither the glory of Truth
Please do not speak of falsehood; that is uncouth

Faith in the Bible, an illusion, a delusion many have said
You will find Truth, too late when you are dead
I understand you wish to die; in living we may have to take a dive
I want to help you see, God, others and yourself how to be alive

Feelings motivate us to action and to muse
Knowledge gives us facts to use
Wisdom is the use of such
The choices of the soul, beliefs do much

Feelings come and feelings go
Perspectives change the facts we know
Wisdom tempers the speed we act
Times change, pain, pleasure its hard to keep our pact
(pact = marriage vows)

Feelings are as weather, blows softly or in gusts
Knowledge is limited to what motivates us

Wisdom is the ability to move according to the truth we known
Actions, our beliefs in motion, what truth embraced is our grow'n

Are you finished with your monologue?
You speak rightly, but life's a fog
To those in pain with burdens to carry
You claim to know, you speak, than to others do you hurry

Life's a war. To live and for a cause to die
Either to self or others, hard to discern between truth and a lie
Pleasure and pain, ignorance, falsehoods obscure right and truth
To ferret out what is what, who, if you can, knows how to sleuth

I feel tormented in my mind
By a demon who creates a double bind
There is no comfort; there is no peace
There is no balm; there is no release

The steel bands about my head
Weigh it down like rings of lead
I see the demon, the pain that he creates
He tries, mocks my convictions, the word of God he desecrates

I cannot escape this torture of the mind
To end it anyway, I can, I am inclined
The visions I see in such clarity
Become inescapable to me

To feel the pain as a coal fire
It is discomfort; to deny it, I would be a liar
I felt betrayed by God above
I felt betrayed by the one I love

He did not do as he said
He set me up to fail instead
He made the world in all its glory
Then life exists, wonder, but it says another story

4

I must work that is OK, I guess
But it never gets done, it's always a mess
My spouse who pledged to love me
A promise from you? It is written of thee

The refusal to be loved hurts as a flame of Hell
The burning sensation, hard to take, express, or tell
That is what you (God) said I know you did
A promise that doesn't deliver, not a man, but a kid

Anger consumes mental energy and focus
Emotion of self-righteousness to locus
So hollow, empty, void of life
The torment of a cancer, strife

Through the pain I learn to hate
I become blind to choices I create
I become dogmatic about my sin
I claim I really have light within

False opinions worth more than gold
All it does is make sin more bold
Where is your love in depths of despair?
Heal this shredded heart, I appeal, beyond repair

There is no peace of mind for me
Condemned to the flame that is me
A drop of mercy would sting like acid
My nerves are lost; my hope is hid

The burning, hollow, painful, lonely, feelings bring tearing
There is no peace, hope, only torment, lonely despair and fearing
Wouldst thou enter with me into the dark abyss?
To feel what I feel, miss what I miss

To know rejection, hand in hand
What sayest thou? Canst thou stand?
Can you see the devils dancing in my mind?
Can you see their mocking glee? How unkind!

Your words of grace, peace and serenity
It creates pain; it is unreal in my reality
I am trapped! No options, pain at every hand
There is no hope, relief, my mind, my grief's demand

My plea there is nothing, I am void of comfort, my torment
What? You have no words of comfort? No? Comment?
Surely your sage advice can be turned to deeds.
I wait in anguish, in despair, who hears my needs?

Demons of the mind
Haunting ghosts of like kind
Specters in the mist
Pain we all feel does exist

In the fog of living shadows
Regardless, of act or not, life still goes
We live and act by our ability
We live by our perceptions of reality

Angels of light we imagine that we call
Devils of night, we see upon the wall
What is real and what is not?
It's hard living not knowing what you've got

Be it good ability in time of woes
Or afflictions in the head to toes
A house of mirrors as I live my life, way unknown
Doors opened, halls closed, even when I'm shown

Discerning glass mirrors and imagined pathways I see
The dead-end, false realities; yet I can touch you and me
In the house of mirrors, fearsome shapes arise
Many mundane, many jump out and surprise

They are many and varied, threatening as I move about
People by the billions all trying to figure this maze out
In the house of mirrors, fantasies enthrall
The tempter shouts, come one come all

They are many and varied, seducing, beckoning me to come
People by the billions all try to follow them, speechless and
numb
The truth about the house of mirrors is it matters not the talk
The truth about the house of mirrors is it matters most the
walk

The truth about the house of mirrors not every way is right
There is but one path that is not illusion and only it will bring
delight

But, everything hurts, even compassion
It tells me then pressure how crushin'
Just to be conscious and conscience is to feel pain
An ounce of love is a pound of hurt, no gain

The "cure" feels worse than the disease
Even if not true, another pain of cold you see
I've become alien to myself
A burning cold, empty labor, a dusty shelf

The injustice I see without
The injustice within a silent shout
End the pain, I want to die, no mistake
Feelings of rejection, by loved ones, are hard to take

In despair, there is no light
In despair, there is no end to night
In despair, there is anguish of pain
In despair, there is no happiness, no gain

Desires of the heart go unmet; life is wearisome, tiring
To continue anyway becomes a crucible firing
The more simple and basic, the desire unmet
The deeper possible the despair, the deeper the pit

What does life consist of in this world?
Upon what are our flags unfurled?
Upon the money that we get?
Upon information granting smiles and making one upset?

Upon the values and images of the mind?
Upon the service we give or receive in kind?
Upon the twitching of the genitals, feelings within?
Upon the touch, the massaging of the skin?

It becomes as nothing, water upon the sand
Fleeting as the notes played by a band
Where is the purpose in the infliction of the pain?
Senseless to create misery, of humanity it is a bane

I feel a drop of rejection hurts like fire
Being wrong hurts as a burn, my rights a funeral pyre
Where do you go when the face of the God of all
Becomes the face of the devil, any options, I find a wall

When all about you is tainted with wrong
Nothing right, but all is evil, I have no song
The piece of God's mind I have is judgment, a hissing
The peace of God's mind, peace, a blessing

Hurts that are physical I'm told are only temporal
But in the spiritual realm such torments are eternal
Join me in my despair and it in the death I'm dying, being boiled
Are you so clean? Are you afraid of being unclean, thus soiled?

Answer me now, please speak, words of comfort please
I will die, if you don't end the pain, I appeal, the pain, appease.

(As the patient spoke the therapist thought
This pain will not go away, may my words be not for naught
It can be dispelled a while, but hides in the shadows
Coming out again another day with bow and arrows)

These painful memories leave scars upon the soul
Only God can cure such pain, heal and make whole
The therapist gently took the patient's hand
Saying no words, it became a fleshly band

Gently spoke, this pain is not an evalution of you
It is not to say your life is through
This pain blinds, can cause impaired thinking
Causes paralysis, so at sin many are winking

What is gained by being bitter towards God?
What really causes pain, yes, but battle not with God
(Their hands slowly parted)

I once plumbed the dark abyss of despair
It's numbing cold, I called help, but none would hear
Is this how God treats those of His salvation?
If this is faith, then I am in defection

I must cure this throbbing pain within
It must leave, so it never comes again
I searched in vain for a cure
But in, why, I found an offered hope to endure

Pain comes from three directions
All due to afflictions and deprivations
When the body doesn't get food, it lets you know, it hurts
When the mind doesn't get satisfied by solutions, it hurts

When the soul doesn't get assurance of love it hurts
When we mistake them for each other, it creates hurts
Why do I want to die? To be with Christ again
When I leave here He greets me, say, "Amen"

The solutions for the body never feed the soul
The solutions for the mind will never make me whole
The solutions for the soul are not met by reason or by space
The solutions for the soul are found by coming to Christ's
place

Sin causes pain, both me to you and you to me
Sin causes blindness in me to you and you to me
Sin causes paralysis in me to you and you to me
Sin causes imaginations of lies in me to you and you to me

Imagined pains mixed with real
Hard discerning the true from the way we think we feel
My pain haunts me every day
It screams, "Thou art in sin and thou shalt pay!"

It seeks to make a prey of me
Another mis-step to drive another arrow into me
Think, man which pains are by my own hand, discern
Which pains are by the hand of others learn

Pain is pain many say, but it is not all true
I can reduce pain by changing, reduce others pain only they
can do
The pain, the weight, and its compression
The pain drives one to a great and dizzying depression

I cannot carry this ponderous weight
It breaks the back, and it is my fate
It is a lonely load to bear
My soul cries within, it is not fair

Would you wish to add to the load of care?
Your words, theirs that make the tempers flare?
Would you wish to bear the grudges you create?
Unforgiving, doubles the load, it triples when you imagine
hate

There are just two things I can give
God's word, by it, and as Job, we die yet we live
Then there is my presence here to give to you
Acceptance, to guide out of wrongs, grant vision to see you
through

The way is long, the night is deep

But there is a God, whose way dost keep

I am spent, I cannot try and I want to die

Let us walk together through this valley of death and
depression

To our doom, in darkness we will be rushin'

Courage, friend, we be dauntless, we walk on even in fear and pain

A fruitless endeavor, a vain hope and nothing to gain

We gain my friend

We gain only death, for that is our end

**Do you do well to be bitter?
If so, it is a petty emotion, like that of a quitter**

*It is not bitterness you see
But pain welling up within me*

This pain a flesh wound, it should heal

A wound of the heart, the condemned eat their last meal

Heart massage can heal it, it will beat pulsating life in your veins

Really now, I suffer time and again, is it all in vain? It has no gains.

**If you do this, what will you tell God?
Your pain was greater than that which His Son suffered, how odd.
The Son took the world's sin, and you but a tiny tiny fraction.
So now you want to die, what is the attraction?**

*Your analogy is off of where it's at
Do not ask questions like that*

**Many have thrown it aside and shut it away
Some did listen and did obey**

*Why?
I still want to die.
Those who have enough. (Emotional support) cannot tell the starving it isn't important to survive
Without this nourishment, surely I shall die, and not be alive*

True of what you say
There are limits on location; brand and timing may cause
delay
This is true, brands do change and payments aren't
forthcoming
It is enough to cause grief and keep our fingers drumming

What I am giving now is one brand of caring
What you were receiving was another, it was erring

(Gun to his temples)
Enough! I take my gun, for I want to die!
I must say you've made a gallant try.

To say good-bye forever, I'll never see this world again
Good-riddance, it's been an ever-increasing pain upon the brain
Good-bye my spouse
This is what you want; death is to be my house

Good-bye my children
Sorry, you see, one destroyed, eaten of grief in a lion's den
Good-bye my friends
You tried to help, but I've become too brittle for life when it bends

Good-bye my God I cannot see
Due to sin, pain and purity of thee
You gave me life, now a life I cannot endure
It's now a mess, for all my efforts, now manure

Now one last good-bye to my dear friend, with whom I speak
Before I pull the trigger, and into death do I peak...

Stop! One last question if I may
For once the trigger's pulled, there is no more day.

Session Two

Ask away I get impatient
In this pain at last I'll make a dent

Before you step into that abyss
Is there not anything you will miss?
We see tragedy and failure; people do crash and burn
We cannot save the world, we must learn

We cannot live the life of others correcting their mistakes
We must, as they, live the consequences of living and its
fates
It is hard to face our own errors of life
Do you wish to compound this by adding to others' strife?

The Devil fogs the way to see
Causing it hard to see God, you, and me
In God's ways we move as if we see in the night
In God's ways we move and see His light

This being true I'll follow God no matter how hopeless, or
"dumb"
I'll follow to death, for it will come
No matter how odd
I'll follow the precepts of God

He made life, shall I end it?
Satan made strife, shall I help it?
There is harmony in following God
Don't bury your talent beneath the sod

So before you go into that abyss
Tell me what you'll miss
I would miss the chance here below
To serve the God of mercy I've come to know

To show His love, learn His word, do my best
Until by His grace He calls me home to His rest
And says, "Well done thou good and faithful servant"
Doing the good and the evil I would help prevent

It is not what I'll miss that counts with me
It is what I would not miss of thee
There is no peace within I said
I would rather die, be dead

End the pain, violence it inflicts, the robbin' crooks
Whether by club or by words, the barbing hooks
There is nothing I can share
For nothing within is good, none do care

It isn't that I blame God above
For I do not doubt His love
It's that I do not believe I'll make a difference
I am a nothing, no peace, no frame of reference

I'll not miss that feeling of being lost and lone
I'll not miss feeling pained and a mere mindless drone
It is the pain I wish to end and step in
With this gun, it can all begin

What assurance have you your pain will end?
What assurance have you peace will descend?
Who told you this is what you get?
Who is he? Have we met?

I hate your words; I'm filled with doubt
How to end the pain I shout
I would end it now if it were not for you
But being honest is what I above all must do
(Patient puts the gun down slowly)

Pain is a fact of life
Some less, some much more strife

What is your cure for life's imperfection?
Bring to my mind a better recollection

Give me your hand and I'll show you the hand of God
          (Patient slowly gives the Therapist other hand)
A bit of His creation, an unseen of what we see abroad

Where did your hand come from?
Open and close your hand some
Who told your brain your hand to move?
It does nothing unless you approve

Is this nothing more than chemicals and electricity?
You choose between the truth, the vain, material and insanity
Did you create the hand you see?
Does your brain really move the hand of thee?

Does the hand that obeys really want your ill
The hand that feeds you, you would kill?
No one denies you feel pain
What is questioned is, is your suicide really gain?

Would a loving God keep you in pain like this?
Sadistically making sure you are amiss?
Satan creates fog to cloud your judgment, deny God's will for life
Making every choice a sin, creating confusion and painful strife

The final question that I ask
Who do you put to task?
The God who loves you for His glory
Or self, and Satan whose end is flaming and quite gory

From Psalms 23 a thought
Words to grant comfort, as they ought
Lo, I walk through the valley of death
Such pain you feel until laid in the earth

I fear no evil for God is with me
This God of comfort, can be true to thee
The Serenity prayer: (Reworded some)
That I can this pain bear

God grant me the serenity to accept the things I cannot change
Change the things I can, those things within my range
And wisdom to know the difference
To know you with love and not offence

Courage to face, strength to act, a plan to move
And humility to walk, and faith to live this hour, thy love prove
I cannot change your pain that is true
But I can be there, a presence to hold you

I cannot change your circumstances, or how things are
But I can help you find or work plans options, near not far
I cannot change the past
But I can show you a future that will last

I cannot change you
But I can show you a path we can walk and be true
The gun of yours until death do you part, this way to cope
With these words I finally say to you, they are words of hope

I cannot find the perfect words, or magic phrases
Or perfect things to do and what amazes
But what I can say, I love you
And do things to show that these things are true

But pain is my companion, a cancer of the soul
It will be ever with me until God makes me whole
Doing God's will will heal
Of the pain I often feel

To ignore God's ways and His appeal
Brings greater hurts from which I reel

What is your pain that runs so deep?
What is your pain that robs you of your sleep?
        (The patient puts down the gun.)

You know not what you ask
You indeed put me to the task
My past regrets of choices lost
Words and actions I didn't count the cost

The penalties they piled high, I've filled up
The bitterness of that drinking cup
There was a time I was you.
My time had come I was through

There was a time says I
When I too wanted to die
Gun to my head
This is it I said

An image came to mind
What reason can justify action of this kind?
Are your sufferings greater than Christ's?
You believe in Him, or you'd be iced.

See the evil in this world
The flag of any doctrine being unfurled
All suppose the will of God
Yet claim His work, cannot work together, how odd

Where is the love that I hear?
Where is the mercy, He claims is near?
This is the hand of mercy my friend said
The hand of God, to keep from a hole in your head

You are sicker than I, to claim that you are God
It is the same if you say you are a cod
He said, it is not I
Listen to the words of God beyond the sky

But the mercy and comfort that I offer
It is yours to take and receive, or be a scoffer
I'm not God, but I saw His merciful hand to mine
I then saw a beam of light, a ray of hope, most sublime

The pain remained, but localized
A chance for hope, I realized
The pain remains in my past
A haunting ghost, I never asked

I see my friend, now and again
We share our joy and our pain
Would you join me in God?
Fighting evil you think so odd

He will grant you some fine day
A new body, the old will fade away
The pains you now deplore
Will vanish away and be no more

The fight for God with His weapons of truth and love
He will guide you with His truth from above
The hand to save you from a sea of sin
Is put forth for you to hold on to from within

Some would say you have lied, and I have truth though you try
I almost believe, I doubt, it is a delusion and a lie

You cannot doubt you can't return
You can't be sure you won't burn
Knowing that you cannot doubt that you do exist
Why imagine pain as this?

You cannot doubt evil exists, if it does then so does good
Good is harmony, tells us to do, as we should
Evil is sin, creating disharmony, making everything gray
Evil would not speak of a judgment day.

You cannot doubt God created this world
Nothing comes from nothing, we are something goes the
herald
God did not create the evil that abounds in this world
Satan started the sin, so out of heaven he was hurled

God says you can, even though you are one
To do the truth that He has begun
You cannot doubt what God calls evil, then or today
That the case why doubt, the good, what the prophets say

Who has a happier, a more contented lot
Those who doubt Jesus, or those who do not?
If God knows all, why did He permit the holocaust of His creation?
To prove to scoffers (Unbelievers) the truth of His revelation

People sight unseen can believe, Him who is supreme
And with His light, faith can beam
Though they die, their faith lives on
In wonder by those who saw them, Truth, Hope isn't gone

A heavy load to bear
How strong is your care

Do not bear your depression's life, all day, an hour, it too is crushing
Sight ahead in depression's life, too dark for you to see, be messing
The light we have is all we need, one step at a time
Clearly seen will keep one from falling from the sublime

A dark maze is life
When we err, it hurts like a knife

We are not concerned with speed, this effort we pursue
It matters not when we reach Heaven; it only matters that we do
We are concerned with how safe and how we do our deed
Are we in the truth, to the hope, in faith, in love of the God indeed?

The way is long, what a plight
The yoke is not easy or light
This cross I have to bear
The way some talk it is no more than air

Pay them no mind
They do not realize they are unkind
Certain perceptions create a double bind
Christ's cross is heavy, not a bit

But note the other burden weighs a greater ton
There is no one to lift it, not God, no one
Each must take their own cross
If they don't, they alone bear that loss

19

Our physical pain determines nothing of who we are
The words of pain we hear, we do not need to bear
We cannot choose the pains inflicted
How to deal with it is often conflicted

What we do can change pain's intensity
Our attitude can change its density

Wounded care for wounded on the battlefield of life
Who is the real enemy, the sinner or comrades in the strife?
I just want to survive in this killing crossfire stream
Turn this nightmare of terror into a blissful dream

I feel a shame that doesn't end
I feel a guilt whose prison bars none can bend
I feel failure, a ceiling I must stoop before
I feel the judgment, the Lord forevermore

I fear the future, destined to be alone I go
Condemned to live in pain, tormenting me here below
The feelings are a constant companion
Driving away any who would be a champion

I cannot seem to function as I would
I have lost the ability, if I could
My self-esteem is gone, such is my fate
Any balm is only a little and now too late

End the pain that shall never die
If it does not then I must try
A paralyzed soul with a mind on the blink
I have lost my dreams I cannot think

End the pain inside of me
I cannot believe I am valued by thee
To live consciously is to live in pain
I have lost my purpose, what do I gain?

Not in terms of money or property
But what am I, to thee or to me?
I have lost and no more entitled to life
End the struggle, end the strife

The battle that rages within the soul
I battle against despair I'm divided, not whole
My future is destined to be flame
I feel it now the present is the same

Never again to feel secure, cozy and good
Locked outside, burning cold, without coat or hood
Forever alone, battlefields unknown
To die bleeding, maimed and alone

Scared forever, if I live day by day
Who gives love to a monster, who are they?
The laws of God are His word
Eternal unchanged, pronounced I heard

I have lost all I hoped to gain to give
Having lost all, I do not wish to live
Parting words again before I use the gun
I grow tired of talk; it is as if you've just begun

I want assurance of intimacy for me to receive
God's law says, "no, at your station" none will relieve.
A burning, I cannot function well
I see myself, going to Hell

Have you really anything more to say
Have you anything from a mysterious they?
Words of God no longer comfort me
Words of promise, feel now cold and empty

I am learning self-hate
My death it cannot really wait.

Session Three

Your hope, your aim to end your pain
To end it anyway you can, these feelings a bane
Would you hope to end the pain in other ways if begun?
That is why we talk, please put down the gun

You love your life, as you should
Mentally, you strive to do and be good
But hooked to mind is our physical sense
Our mind upset, pain is hard to put hence

Be not obsessed with sense stimulation
Pleasure too, like pain, distorts true evaluation
We forget God in either case
That is a situation potentially most base

To love God and appreciate His creation
Treat others with love (Agape) without trepidation
You have seen others make it through
It would be nice if another would be you

Having known this, you find words you try
Express yourself, find a way not to die
This you believe can be done to this end
So at last in life you can find a friend

You have a strong desire for vindication
You want your guilt cleared by absolution
Not being God I cannot grant this thing
Tragically, it will add to pain another string

In this our talk you do hope
I hope too, so we can cope
This faith we have and do share
This is what shows we do care

It is hard to live with hollowness of heart
When inside echoes, you are not as thou art
Pain that never dies
Hope that fails when it tries

Nightmares haunt the day
Daydreams in the night fade away
A hollow echo I am alone
The fellowship shared is gone

Silent tearful sorrows
Joy slips from my tomorrows
Bleeding inflammation of the heart
Useless first aid to impart

Continued abandoned alone soul
Salvation lost, a divided whole
Despair lives and does thrive
My faith is much more dead than alive

Apathy always and again
Love has yet to begin
Darkness with no effort does prevail
Light flickers, goes out, to no avail

Death's triumph song
Life's bloody battle, lost gone
Here is an agonizing paradox
This is Satan's tool that sly fox

To stay, this hurts like a flame of Hell
Heal the pain; turn back on God; that is where I shall dwell
But an effort to deny my Lord
That is a thing I cannot afford

Keep the hurt and do His will
Than my cup, his overflowing fill
Maintain God's honors, or face His wrath
End of story, end of life's path

Elements of this world melt away
God's resurrection glory is here to stay
After all I have said and done
I feel I have lost, and Satan has won

I have come to wonder why
What assumptions, problems have I?
Why do I have them, what are they?
What questions to find them, what to say?

Who do I believe and why?
What do I believe, I cry?
Must I rebuild from ground zero?
Rebuild again, shows me a failure not a hero

What are my spouse's feelings and assumptions and beliefs?
What will ever bring healing and relief?
How do I answer questions if I not only not know how
But may not want to know from the future or now

I may not want to know, and not know it, even if I should
I may not want the answer even if I could
Why the answer I fear is more painful than ignorance I feel
If such is the case, may mean, I could know, would I heal?

This is true then it isn't the truth, I fear it is the pain
Once the truth is known, one must live it, or loses the gain
Live it within the laws that God has set
Not to is to compromise the truth we have met

There is a certain responsibility with truth and self
Some forego the pain and put this on the shelf
There is more anger than I realized was here
This is simmering with the other things I hold dear

With this pain as it is I feel at times, I am not my name
I can distance myself then I ask, why I came
He is either better or worse than me
But I do not know, ask "my" name who is he?

A desire to remarry, but if I am him
I cannot marry again, and the end estate is so grim
Bound to a vow, even my spouse does not honor it
My self-esteem, shot, do it I must, fool? Or true grit?

Emotional energies oppose the mental on the field
Each are strong, neither will yield
Feign that I am Hell bound already in my destiny
Self-hate runs high, for errors that I did not see

Applying solutions to misinterpreted problems and mistakes
How do I make right the errors, heal the pains and aches?
I feel suffocating drowned in an ocean of depression
Immersed, hard to move, mind in a slow motion

Short-circuited, reasoning, no map to locate it
I just keep going, hoping just to make it
A pipe dream if I may
A forbidden dream is that O.K.?

To be called up in front of the church
We have a wife for you; you are not left in the lurch
I would be married to a chosen woman for me
Well formed to my ambitions and desires of thee

And I to hers, it would be so
Documentation that this marriage could go
The time of service makes no difference
I would have off the next week for my reference

Why is this the way for me today?
I cannot choose, the last I was made to pay
I cannot choose this wife this time
The last I chose was not sublime

Nothing lavish first time we met
She knew of me, and what she'd get
She would want me, that is true
She would my dreams fill through

25

We'd be taken to a hotel I had supposed
Then we'd draw the curtains closed
Why this pipe dream cannot occur instead
I cannot remarry as I said, the vow wasn't broken in the bed

It would never be arranged without me in this way
I am to be responsible, the way we do things this day
My church would not approve of this choosing
Not the woman, the mechanism is losing
      (There are not anymore, "matchmakers")

People think it outdated, God is silent on this matter
How we choose is not a concern of the latter
There is no peace like a river
Instead a cold vision that makes me shiver

God has written He removes the branches not bearing fruit
Is she removed to be replaced? Or is that question moot?
By another woman in my life?
Is another destined to be my wife?

But this would go against the vows we made
The things we said to do to make the grade
What God joins let not man/woman put asunder
What God joins, God can divide with thunder

It would be presumptuous to suppose this is the case
For she believes that I am guilty, the one most base
I cannot live on this way
What is the solution I must pray

I have no peace from day to day
What is the price I must pay?
I cannot endure the flames I feel
I repeat myself, the pain I reel

The Therapist (thought)
How do I touch the pulse of humanity?
How do I get beyond the heredity?
How do I get through the vanity?
How do I get him to see the validity?

How do I console the broken heart?
Where do I begin, where do I start?
How to touch the shattered glass of soul?
Where is the skill to repair the goal?

How to mend what is not there?
How to sew the rend, the tear?
How to save one drowning in grief?
How do I, Lord, send relief?

The lifeline of words I send out to you
Are very thin threads, they break, they do not do
These feeble and weak words I've got
Lord, help me to reach him lest it be for naught

His will is beyond my reach
For different reasons we do screech
For a lost soul I do mourn
He seems lost, forgotten and forlorn

Help me to rekindle the fires of belief
Grant it not be a funeral fire of grief
Am I God to grant peace and recovery?
Am I to sight the blind and to truth possibility?

Therapist (speaks)
The devil provides imaginary provocation pains
The devil provides how it is we are to make gains

As the pains gets worse
I want a hearse
Believe truth or lie
Believe the wrong and I shall die

It is increasingly hard to live
Even to let pain pass, like water through a sieve
There is only one painful solution
That is Godly, duty and devotion

How can another bear my pain?
To think that they can, is it not in vain?
Our support groups, self-help groups, I've read
They are pallbearers for each other being dead

In bitterness many try to show whom is boss
To do so seems to be a vanity and a loss

Therapist (thought)
I cannot touch the burn victims, of human will
Judge who is right and wrong, my words go still
The balm of despair, is hope, beyond hope
To get him to Thee he needs tools to cope

Therapist (speaks)
My presence is all I have, I'm sorry for your pain
The fact that I cannot help is my bane
I wish to help you clean up emotional pollution
That is my work, my resolution

I became thus so involved
Thus so I am resolved

Another feather in your cap
Or am I no more than just a patient that?

I cannot bear your unbelief
If you wish to take your life like a thief
Be my guest and have it done
For doing it you believe that you have won

I do not think it right
Your thinking has taken flight
Yes, you have your reason, that is true
Is it the pain, or is it you?

God made us, and He doesn't create junk
It is man that messes up and made it stunk
He created you for a purpose true
Trite, but special, are you

Priceless beyond worth is your soul
Jesus died to assure, heaven is your goal
Actions we do not, or actions we do
All add up for good or evil they do accrue

Those in Jesus will lead to heaven, and our heart doth swell
Those outside will lead to the outside darkness, Hell
Times do change, this is true for all people far and near
God's truth does not, and He is in control so do not fear

You paint a pretty picture with your words that God is nigh
But there are some things that do not color, that's why I sigh
The pain goes on despite assurances from you
The pain goes on in me through and through

It does not quit with drugs, or drink, or activity I see
It does not quit with prayer or time, I say to thee

I understand what you say
I will not quote, a group or a they
Please understand this action you will regret and despair
Look to the future, you will see, you cannot this bridge repair

There is more than one bridge that cannot be repaired
The marriage or other things I have now despaired
My past is gone, is shot, there is no return
So now my life I do burn

What you say certainly has a ring as far as it goes
But please remember, you have to see beyond your nose
Yes, you hurt beyond the words you've spun
Healing of this kind takes time even when just begun

It goes to the heart infects the blood
It corrupts the soul, it returns to mud

This is the pain that talks and wants relief
To keep it going retain your unbelief
On judgment day your works and struggle become known
This could be a time for you to shine, your courage be shown

With all due respect to God above
I do appreciate His love

But it does not take one to have courage to feel pain
Losers have pain and nothing is all they gain.

Session Four

Your words again are only true as far as they go
The perspective is not right, as right as you could know
The loser has pain, so he quits, this no denying
The winner has pain; the winner keeps on trying

Even if the winner never makes the grade
He can say he tried with sweat and blood he paid
The loser cannot even make that claim
He usually tries to find another to blame

The winner will keep at it because it is right
The winner will keep going even in the night
The winner will consider the context of his choice
The winner will consider the authority if the voice

The winner changes, but doesn't stop
The winner will re-consider and learn from the flop
The loser will stop, can call it wrong to go
The loser will stop and figure I can't truly know

The loser will only think of actions, not morality
The loser will only consider a voice he likes, not reality
The loser changes, not for the reason he ought
The loser doesn't learn through lessons taught

Calling me a loser will not help the pain go away
Nor will it help me cope, the pain is here to stay

There are others' whose lot is worse than you

Fine, then, you talk to them, to me as you do

You still hurt; that is clear
Our time is over; the end is near

As I said to others, you do go
I am the same, no change in pain you know

The gun you will have to leave it behind

Do yourself a favor, leave it here, it would be kind

There is no answer, to the pain I have inside?
Is there no balm, with me it ever dwells, it does abide

Hope does not reduce the pain you feel?
Hope assured does not help and heal?

It would if there was something there
There is nothing that can do the care

The hope the Bible speaks of, does it not to you?
Can you not give the writer of the Bible His due?

The hope of the Bible speaks of isn't new
I have lost the feel for what the Bible says is true
What I want will not help the pain away
What I want is a second chance, another day

There is one thing I can do, for all of what it is worth
I can talk with you about your second birth
I can be with you when you talk about your trouble
I too do not live inside a bubble

To talk about pain and speak of it does some good
As long as you see some light, you can do what you should
We'll talk again when we can
We will talk again man to man

I am sorry for your hurting soul
It is only when new love is found that healing can begin

That is a new chapter I cannot write just yet today
The pain is overpowering, the price of healing I cannot pay
I hope a solution will come before I fall forever
If I do not see you, you will not hear from me ever

Let us talk about it and other things in this hour
Let us seek and find, the words will grant us power

I shall return some day to be sure now I think
You shall not like my pain, from me you shall shrink

You let that be my burden, you do not have to carry
The pain you bear is heavy, you do not have to hurry
This life is not a race, for what are you competing?
Life is more than a job, clothing or what you are eating

Life is precious so I give you some last bit of a word
Seek another out, share your life. It will help heal I have heard

Very well, I will not die today
The pain still exists, help me find another way
The way is hard, and I want to die
End the pain anyway, I will try

I was alive once in my past
It is tragic it did not last
To one to share my life and pain
You did not say marriage, I trust again

To share living is not easy to do now
To describe the feelings I still ask myself, how?
There is no glory in this story, this account
There is no gain in my pain, of no amount

There are no words I can give you
There are no actions I can do
I am lost, a wounded soul
I feel raised high on a pole

To leave you it seems I must
But I'll not leave in a cloud of dust
I'll trudge along at a slow pace
Unable to look up at any face

I am gone; my strength is spent
I will go now though my soul is bent
Only God can fix this wound I have if He may
I hope it will be fixed before judgment day

I give you my assurance; I'll not use the gun
My words are spent; they are done
I'll return; we will talk again; I'll grasp the rope
We will find a way for me to cope

Until I have found this future of which you illustrate
I will mark the time, in your advice, until I find a date.

Session Five

Please say on continue pray
Describe the pain that haunts you night and day

There is no peace
There are no feelings of release
It burns, the fears of the soul
I am a nothing; it takes its toll

It comes; I pay a heavy price
It is cold, a burning cold, like ice
My mind says it not so
Prove it says feelings, or go

My failures say feelings prove it true
You are a nothing through and through
We are witnesses and your ex-wife too
She wouldn't lie; your deeds do accrue

Yet, my mind says it isn't so
We have a heart; we can grow
We fail 'tis true, but it isn't the end
My past mistakes, I can mend

Unforgiving, you'll pay at last (you meaning the patient)
Now I'll call you to task
Now I flounder in the feelings of losses
Nothing but dreams that the tempest tosses

What was once a nightmare, now a reality
Now those hopes, a fading memory
I want to die, and end it all
I wish to end the pain, end its call

You have dreams, and heart that beats
You know the song and life's treats
You can sing again there is hope once more
There will be a land, a person to adore

You torment me with pie in the sky
Please don't tell me such a lie

But it is true if you raise your hope's desire
Yes, it hurts, it burns, you must go through the fire
The hopes you have, a guiding light
That is your strength in this your fight

The feelings you have indeed are strong
But you can if you step upon step, and right the wrong
In the end it will not matter
It doesn't matter what people chatter

In the end the only words that count
Are those from God, the word from His mount
Those words we all long to hear
"Well done my servant!" from God does us cheer

Fix your dreams in your mind
Repair the thoughts, as you are not blind
Move the thoughts to kind action
Prepare then for faith's activation

Pray to God in heaven above us all
He will enable you to walk tall
Not vengeful, arrogant, unloving, unkind, prideful ability
But gentle, merciful, loving, compassionate humility

It isn't that I distrust God, I've said before
I distrust myself, with all my trying, I am sore
My strength is spent and I am gone
I feel I don't to Him belong

It isn't how you feel that counts with Him
It is based on promise, faithful, and His light is never dim

It isn't the God above I doubt of thee
It is with people who do not want me
My pressures I will mention
Maybe you can add a "proper" dimension

As I said before I cannot marry forevermore
The way is locked, bolted as a sealed door
Until she dies, I cannot marry
I must be celibate, until one of us they bury

Then there is the selling of my talent
Employers always find fault I am lament
I cannot sell well especially when sad
Employers see this, not this man, not this lad

So also now the pressure by the drive for sex
I'm pressured to get a job next
I cannot live well this life I've got
Condemned to live upon the cot

You cannot overturn the law God laid down
To do so you would have to lie, and God would frown
What comfort can you give me?
Even if I try, try as busy as a bee

It comes to nothing, no employer wants me
I have no selling skills it is apparent don't you see

You make a case most eloquent indeed
You know your doctrine and your creed
You have a moral standard high
No doubt you will carry it 'til you die

I cannot free my mind from these hunger pains
Seductive women and dollar signs, their need gains
I am not greedy please understand from this
This is survival, not luxury, or life I miss

This isn't a matter of martyrdom
But simple facts of life as they come
If the church knew my feelings, if they were aware
I am sure they'd stare, stare, stare

If there were a purpose to this madness
Then maybe, just maybe, I could endure this sadness

I am sold by what you've said
But it is no good if you are dead

And it does no good to take it before God Almighty
Do you think I can answer Him all rightly?

Perhaps a petition is what you need
God is merciful in word and deed

Then does God permit pain without remedy?
Senseless violence, music without melody?

Why does God keep you in this bind?
Why people don't or can't help, how unkind
Are those the questions in your mind?
Do you want answers, is that what you hope to find?

Suppose I do and you explain
That sounds nice, but I'll disdain
I'll guess the answer is not what I desire
But end the pain, for that I'll hire

I'll explain, as I am able to
Thank you for your honesty, that is true
Pain comes and pain goes as does pleasure
It comes in work and in leisure

Physical pain tells us something is wrong with us
Pain of soul is just as wrong, which many cuss
Our actions in handling of pleasure and pain
Tells us of the soul within we choose blessing or bane

The only reason I can say this to you
The Bible for you must be adhered to
To others who have no concept of right and wrong
They'd be content with a drink and a song

A bit farfetched perhaps to say so now
But they are not as minded as thou
The Devil has a choice too
To try you time and again through and through

Especially those he hasn't got
Because he hates those who would not rot
What happens to us is incidental
How we choose to act counts, it is not all mental

We are judged by God based on what we do with what we got
Judged by intent, thought, actions, and words count, do they not?
Our judgment based on what we did in faith believing on Him
Not based on fame, fortune, merit or the body from the gym

The outward appearance may look the same
But inwardly, our action is in whose name?
Pain/pleasure comes as a result of several things
By our hand, others and/or by what chance brings

Whatever comes your way
Our Duty is to give God the day (Ecc. ch 12)
To end your pain I cannot do
Understanding can keep it from controlling you

What helps to ease the pain is this
A warm touch, share, another human bless
Focus on God and awareness of life and what it senses
Conscious of what you bless and what are your offenses

Pain can encourage blinding bitterness, hatred and despair
Pleasure can encourage apathy, need for God will need repair
There is pride in each hazard to man
Work day by day, on what you can, that is the plan

Care not for the judgment of others
It is God that counts, not cousins, family, sisters, brothers
What is the purpose to this pain cycle you behold?
Silence the devil, his charges on you be bold

God will be with you in your choice
As long as He can bless your action and rejoice
Your righteous life will silence him forever
Just be sure, make pleasing God your endeavor

There is the pain of hers, it isn't just me
Her pain too is great, can't you see?
I can't help her from her bleeding heart
I can't offer healing or balm impart

She wants me out today and now
But I cannot ignore my vow
One image then another on my mind
I cannot respond well to pain of this kind

The female beauty now forbidden to me
Man was created this way before the tree
I move out because it will please her today
In the end I know I will surely pay

My thoughts are jumbled and run together
I cannot untie the mass of thought, it just gets tighter
The feelings of acid on my soul
Cause the unheard voice to howl

Again I wraith in pain to die
This keeps up I'll have to try
My thinking then will not care about the future
The wounds too deep & ripped for any surgeon to suture

The sea of emotion overwhelms me
The pull to the riptide is too great for me

Let me be and die in shame
We all know I am to blame
Despite the fact I can't name a sin
I must have done a cruelty within

Therefore I must pay the price and die
She will feel better, I bet for joy she'll cry
I cannot bear the pain I've said before
Nor can I hear your words anymore

Let me die a death of a fool
That I am, let the jackals drool
Had I not the mind I do
Surely I would have followed through

I now bow to your word
None can end; your advice will sound absurd
The pain goes on, it does not stop
I feel all day that I must drop

The Bible gives a hollow message to me
I am now in bondage* I'll never be free
*(Being the sex drive, and desire for intimacy and doctrine
forbidding marriage)

We have been over this ground before
We can go over it again and say more

I must die, what more to say?
I must have done badly to this day
I am in deep depression, this I know
So to my death I will go

I cannot live today in pain
Living each day is but in vain
There is not a way to get over the feeling
You know not with what I am dealing

The flames of Hell, lick heart and feet
The emptiness, the cold, despair, and defeat
I have lost my self-esteem to thee
Let me die, please let me be

I cannot carry on the feast of death, my repast
When I ate to the full, I regret, my hopes, tried my best
I've lost hope as she has said
I've done her wrong; I have been bad

I've failed her and now I pay
To Hell I go on this fine day
No one can help me in my distress
No one can pull me from this mess

Little if anything in my life has value
It is now payment time; it's overdue
No funds for which to pay my debt (emotional)
I've met my match, bankrupt is what I get

I cannot put the pieces back together
My hopes and dreams are broken by bad weather
They've been destroyed, despite my effort, I am shot
Now to go to where it is ever hot

I'm given to despair, loss of hope
I doubt you've words, so I can cope
There is nothing to say to this
Except good-bye to endless bliss

I'm marked a failure now for life
My job is low; I'm divorced by my wife
There is no peace as I have said
That being said I am better off dead

I cannot function without a loving wife
I need a companion for sharing life
It is hard to live with hollowness of heart
When inside echoes, you are not of thou art

Pain that never dies
Hope that fails when it tries
Nightmares haunt the day
Lovely dreams they fade away

A hollow echo alone
The fellowship is gone
Silent tearful sorrows
Joy slips from tomorrows

Bleeding inflammation of the heart
Useless, first aid to impart
Continued abandoned soul
Salvation lost, a divided whole

Despair that does thrive
Faith is more dead than alive
Apathy always and again
Love has yet to begin

Darkness with no effort
Lights flicker, go out to no avail
Death's triumph song
Life's bloody battle lost and gone

Duty to God's honors, or face His wrath
End of story, end of path
Elements of this world melt away
God's resurrection glory here to stay

Ssshh, quiet, say no more
Yes, I know you've said it all before
Ssshh quiet, please say no more
Just sit a minute, or two, quiet I implore

Say nothing, not a word, no more
For now settle, rest, I know you are very sore
No one questions the pain you are in
No one denies your emotions beneath your skin

No one says your heart is not as flame
Please do not give or fix blame
Try to step outside the situation that you feel
We'll discern together the imagined and the real.

Before I go on, please be assured
I know your pain is highly pressured
I know it burns red hot
I know it burns all you've got

Only a memory of what you planned
Clouds now gone, blown to another land
The negative statements you relayed to me
I relay the problems back to thee

"I must die"
Focuses on the wrong, the false is in your eye
I do not know, I do not know
Translates into I do not want to know

The translation of I have, has no option
It is a blindness to what I could have begun
I am ill or sick inside
That will surely, surely, set your health aside

I am in torment in pain
This is magnified and will drive insane
How much I want to die
Focus on this, and you get an attitude that won't try

"I hate myself and so I cannot go on"
Amplifies our sorrow to death, so life is gone
Change the focus of self-speak
Then other possibilities you can greet

I must live to this I cleave
This gives determination I believe
I know I can find out
This seeks to end ignorance we can do without

I have options I can choose
Opens resources so I can work and not lose

I have health and live well, rather than a dry well
This creates water and an attitude of hope does swell
I am aware of limitations
I am a realist for overcoming situations

How much I want to complete my goals
This attitude provides a drive for our souls
I love myself this is true
I have things to do for Christ and for you

I feel I cannot do the things that you said
I still feel I'd be better off dead
The fighting waves is too hard for me
I am drowning in my emotional sea

Lifeboats of reason cannot save?
Can no one shine a light into your cave?

Only the touch of human love
That I can trust in faith the peace, the dove
I want absolution for my "crime"
I want a remarriage most sublime

But neither can be granted to me
Except by God, He is key
But He cannot, bound by His word
Unless He violates that which is absurd

Is He not a God of mercy?
Would He not extend something to thee?
God helped Naomi and Ruth
Will he not help you in truth?

Yes, He helped those people through
But they did not sin, and could marry too

I know it must be hard
There are others, do not disregard
David who could marry this is true
Would you want to bear what he went through?

There is Job, and Lazarus, and the apostle Paul
There are others, these are not all
Our emotions are like weather it comes and goes
Regardless of our understanding, our maps, of how it blows

Our mental light of knowledge does not help the best
**Our light is feeble within ourselves, so to God we make
request**
The true light within a troubled heart
It is the word of God, His wisdom does impart

Regardless of the weather, or light that we see
His word will guide us safely into eternity
If we refuse the advice His word does give
We will in the end, forfeit the life we would live

My world has collapsed, and now to rebuild amidst the flame
I want to feel good about myself again, never mind who's to blame
My world lies in ruins, with nothing, how do I rebuild the life
Just the bunkers that I use to hide, survive the pending strife

I cannot rebuild without a partner to share the work
Without such a one "play" or "work," I will go berserk
Being that this is what I am now denied
I feel as though someone has lied

A troubling thing to think
But anyway, I cannot stand, so I sink

At least there is a place you can go
There I plead you consider this and grow
In your bunkers, make your plan, with this in mind
Consider, if I condense what I said, please be kind

The words I said could be summed this way
Think I can, make your plan, and be sure to play.

Session Seven

Do you still want to die?

I still want to die says I

Surely in staying alive you can see a gain

Not when everything I do is pain
I travel in the park
Every voice wants me to hark

I do good and right, as I should
I smile and bow as I could
But there is an empty hole
To have it filled is my goal

It is not filling a mere cavity
The loss of her, a personality
The two become one, one a whole
Lose the one; it becomes a hole

There is a pain worse than no wife
That is the pain of no life
Now I feel I am without both
The marriage broken and the oath

I have no place to go really, I can find
There is no place, so I am in a bind
The one thing I have received from thee
You have been here to listen to me

A hope that there may yet be a way
A single ray of hope, to find a day
For now though the night is here
My concerns become many a fear

In talking to you I have come to wonder, why?
What assumptions cause this desire to die?
Why do I think that death is what I want to have?
Take the pain away, put on the salve

What are these feelings, that come so strong?
They are powerful, for right or wrong
What questions do I ask to find out why?
I must answer them or I die

Who do I believe? Why would I do it?
What do I believe? Why would it be legit?
Must I rebuild from ground Zero?
My spouse's feelings? I'm a failure, not a hero

Her assumptions, why must I know?
They hurt time and again, blow for blow
Even in pain I am aware
I find I shy away from right and fair

Keeping the faith is most painful. And rest cannot mend
If I leave for sinful comfort, I stand condemned
To end the pain it is such a nature within
I'd confess to almost any crime, real or what I imagine

The pain is like keeping back the sea
The tide of emotion is too much for me

Pain may give pleasure we can't see
When it comes time to leave, many say let me be
Pain can turn to bitterness and self-righteous hate
We don't want to give it up, what then is our fate

We feel better about doing painful things
We feel better if we can feel a sting
Righteousness will not keep tragedy at bay
Job was righteous, but tragedy had the day

Remember what is God's will in context
Is not His will, in another or the situation next
Job's righteousness is not based on money before God
Lazarus's righteousness is not based on lack of money before
God

The desire you have isn't as wrong as many say
The desire you have will likely stay
It is a particular desire that makes it bad
It is the unlawful desire, of what another had

The devil in our life, many times is our own sin
It comes back to haunt us, regrets memories within
To excise the demons, sin less and do not dwell there
They will return to tempt you, this time you are aware

You know they are coming and what they are about
You then will not tremble at their whisper, or their shout

How do I know which questions to ask?
That is an assignment, a burdensome task
The questions do not come, there seems to be a block
Are these to be said against a clock?

There is a block of sorts says I
Questions too, answer them before you die

What is the block to my mind?
Emotion, truth, I cannot face the double bind
The answer if I knew may be more painful than I want to know
Must I know it in order to grow?

Ignorance feels better, and there is less pain
It seems that I can get a better gain

That is illusion; you will not grow, but become dull of mind
You will find other ways to hide yourself, then become unkind

I fear having to live a reality that is most painful for life
There is no way to cut out the problem, amputate with a knife
To live this way daily is hard enough to overcome
When others say pat answers to pain, I gnash teeth and am dumb

I must live within the life that God has set
I hope to live, within the conditions and have them met
It is by His grace I live the life I have
His salvation, oh please let it not be the only salve

There is such a hollow echo within my soul
It burns, it's heavy, it's black as coal
Do not give me platitudes of how I will live it through
Of advice sayings, and how it will make you stronger too

You are right, wisdom will not make up for your sorrow
It can give a better understanding, maybe hope for tomorrow
Distractions when in this frame of mind, cost is heavy, what they buy
They become a narcotic, additive, blinding, but they deny

It supersedes what God says is really right
To end the pain, their "god," their plight
Security from God that is what you really want, your goal
To see His providence, and end the anguish of the soul

Faith comes to those who reach out in faith, believe that He is
God will reward those who do, at that He is a wiz
We believe because of who God is, we, the products of His creation
He lets us know and He can, believe then His resurrection

Now we need understand God's part, and our part of faith is seen
Today the blessings that He gives, to those whose sight is keen
God will provide you with an answer if you look with his eyes
You must work with what He has, only then will He bless you realize

That is a pat answer if I ever heard one

I suppose you wish to trust your gun?
There are still those who will sit with thee
I will sit, and watch, will you with me?

The pain is deep, this I know
I have had it too, I told you so
I also know in my conviction of whom I know
God will provide an answer for loss, so you can go

Some call it coincidence, chance, you get a blessing
It is God saying, I know, I am coming, reassuring

Some would say it is a delusion of the mind's eye
Others say, a promise of pie in the sky

They can say what they will and want; they talk like geese
But I know God will provide you security, calm and your
peace

It will come in a way of God's choosing
When it does, don't be snoozing
It may not be what you expect to see
Be assured it is the blessing of God on thee

I will try what you have suggested
I believe I will the devil in my life bested
I will do what the Lord would have me do
I will be patient, for God would have time too

This pulsating pain runs to the marrow of the bone
God please deliver me, and call me your own
I faint while I wait here for thee
Please wait with me

That was why I want to die
It isn't over though; it burns like lye
The hope that God delivers on what He said
It is a hope I wouldn't find me dead

Lord, bring your solution
Grant me absolution
I cringe that I will lose my best security I know
I believe you will grant me something better, please don't say no

Amen!

Session Eight

These thoughts go on without in a circle
That they may stop would be akin to a miracle
My self-esteem is gone; such is my fate
Any balm is only a little and now too late

End the pain that shall never die
If it does not then I must try
A paralyzed soul with a mind on the blink
I have lost my dreams, I cannot think

End the pain inside me
I cannot believe I am valued by thee

To live consciously is to live in pain
I have lost my purpose, what do I gain?

Not in terms of money or of property
But what am I, to thee, or me?
I have lost no more entitled to life
End the struggle, end the strife

The battle that rages within the soul
I battle against despair; I'm divided, not whole
My future is destined to be flame
I feel it now the present is the same

Never again to feel secure, cozy and good
Locked outside, burning cold, without coat or hood
Forever alone on battlefields unknown
To die, bleeding, maimed alone

Scared forever, if I live
Who would to a monster love give?
The laws of God are as His word
Eternal unchanged, and pronounced I heard

I have lost all I hoped to gain to give
Having lost, I do not wish to live
Parting words again before I use the gun
I grow tired of talk it is through, as though you've just begun

I want assurance of intimacy my way (coming towards me)
But God's law says "No, now in your station stay"
A burning I cannot function well
I see myself going to Hell

Have you really anything more to say?
Have you anything from a mysterious they?
Words of God do not comfort me
Words of promise feel cold and empty

A prayer that I prayed hard to my Lord
A prayer that cuts me like a sword
Heavenly Father Holy art Thou
Unto thee in prayer, I humbly bow

My petition do I make
Knowing only thou can give and take
Deepen my knowledge of your word
Thou grant wisdom to me I have not heard

My cross is heavy for me to bear
Would you grant me a loving wife, always there?
The one who is now, now sends me away
I am as dust, a heart of stone, and feet as clay

Can I endure this time on earth alone?
And not sin, a sin and defile your holy throne?
You are bound by your word and me a vow
You have wisdom, love and rule as now

One who would help me bear the load of old
Our comfort to each other, your will unfold
Forgive the sins I cannot see
For it is they that will be the death of me

Forgive the sin, I'm ashamed to confess
The humiliation to say it is I who made this mess
Forgive I pray who sinned against me
I cannot go on alone from thee

I'm sorry for the sin where I have pride
They mock my God, and Jesus who died
I appeal to you for hope
Grant me ears to hear so I can cope

Forgive the heart when I have coveted what I should not
My heart is hurting, wanting, despairing what I haven't got
In Jesus name I pray to thee
Knowing only then, I can be me

A heartfelt prayer
Soul's emotion more than air

There is no peace, only torment of the mind
If peace came, I wouldn't see it of any kind
My words are a fraction of what I feel to me
The words I want elude me; they flee

My pain becomes heavy to a great degree
What I want is to bend your will to agree with me
I want to puzzle out the phrases and the word
To persuade your mind by what you heard

By this effort of finding a solution
You would or will be mine granting absolution
But I know that, even if I were to succeed
My pain would remain, a self-deceiving deed

The pat answers that crowd my mind
Mock at me and are most unkind
Just pray more and you will be all right
Just pray more and things will be bright

Have more faith and you will get what you request
Have more faith, you shall receive, search for your quest
Be anxious for nothing said our Lord and receive
He grants us all things, so believe

Bible people of old handled things like this
So be like them, their faith can't miss
Our pain is only a little while then we die
So have faith, you will get it if you try

There are those worse off than you
Complaining is not what you should do
It is the will of God for you to suffer so
But faith in God, live and God will make you go

Count your blessings, not your pains
For in them you will find your gains
Do church work, occupy the mind and soul
Do His will; it will make you whole

This time of trial will make you stronger
Endure faith; it won't last much longer
The quotes have a hollow ring
Yet they all believe it is just the thing

Pleasantly they live, sing and dance
I have only loneliness, no comfort, no chance
Helping others and the pain will heal
I do, but I find in the end that is no lasting deal

The pain returns and stronger too
I am finding such it's necessarily true
It may help in others' time of need and solution
For me it won't help, nor grant absolution

I fear God terrorized by judgment, under the gun
This is for all the things I thought or have ever done
I fear getting beaten up for being me
What offense, never mind, guilty thou shalt be

Fear, never measuring up enough to work, it's a thing I can't hack
I never could get a better job, because there is a thing I always lack
My marriage, I never earned enough
Fear of the same at work, it makes it tough

The 2nd marriage (?) I am marked now
She "threw" me out; it matters not the why or how
She refused the plan to make things better
Why, it seems, doesn't really matter

After I got married, a happy key
I found I failed, failed, failed, and life will not be forgiving me
Neither will God's word, for I cannot marry again
Feelings of salvation lost, it is a bitter pain

I cannot live with a companion; that is adultery
I would burn forever; I feel now eternity
A joyless life and contentment lost
A debt I owe, I counted the cost

I cannot tell you how close to death I feel
I preferred to live, but without a loving wife, I reel
Irrational, no possibility to love again as before
It is lost now forevermore

That possibility is now blocked for life
Hurts more, the blessed say I must live in this strife
If I could "be allowed to marry" to which it is a pain buffer
Many would say I am too "sick," no marriage, so suffer

There is no way I can ignore the "suffering" for now
The broken things are my failure somehow
The spiritual deprivation of the soul
I feel broken I cannot be made whole

Saying heaven is worth the price
Offers no comfort from those who have it nice
From those who do not, or haven't paid this cost
The emotional perspective, my salvation, it is lost

It is an ever-present pain to me
Would I recognize healing? No to be honest with thee
I want to be healed, yes I do
But I am blind to it, so I am through

I would not feel good about Jesus in my house; I'd feel dumb
He would find a joyless place, would he really want to come?
A broken heart, a failure, no peace and fear of Hell
My only future, all actions, fruitless, as a dry well

If a woman I do get
She'd be happier if we hadn't met
I would fear I'd repeat the failing I have now
Once again repeat the failure I knew not how

I tremble to see the wisdom of the Lord
I tremble to see the sword of the Lord
I tremble to the light
I cower beneath the power of His might

To think that wisdom that made the cycles
The world systems, interactions and its miracles
If life can see itself and in the Creator's mind
It would catch a glimpse of glory most sublime

Temptations strike again, I failed, I believe
Condemned to sin no matter the effort I give, I grieve
A constant sense of condemnation
A haunting cloud, there the feelings of humiliation

I feel I cannot walk on the sunny side of the street
For that is where the saints walk, and where they meet
The only thing worse than a fool, which I am
Is a dead fool, better alive, I hope, and learn I can

God has no pleasure in the death of the wicked, or a fool
So I must live as I can, try to avoid the sin and its drool
Alas each day will be like the one before
Each day's sunshine, birds sing, and I am sore

I will go on, no change, and forced to be alone
Forced celibacy, no relief, but sin God doesn't condone
I feel my heart turning to stone then to steel
The devil then offers a sinful deal

I feel beyond the reach of God
I am yet bound by vow; some think that is odd
Christ did no miracle on the human will
Nature, demons, resurrection, he commanded they did the bill

Armchair Christians advise the down and out
Their gifts help, but real comfort is missing in what they tout
Material blessings given, thank you, for these who can see
They cannot touch the soul that's crushed and feels cast from thee

My life is lived in fear, not confidence or faith
I have lost connection between me and "...the Lord saith"
Yet I must do my duty blind as I am as God said
Hopeless or not, if I stray more, I would be truly dead

There is no peace that I can see
There is no hope, what can you offer me?
I live in a maybe hope, for God is one of mercy
A father who notices, yet, will grant a blessing in my adversity

You seek escape, not from life, but from pain
In your efforts, you will lose more than you gain
Many seek the same goal as you; either choice has its price
Some seek, like you, virtue, but many more seek vice

Pain keeps us from loving this world
Be ready for the next, when its flag is unfurled
Your trouble is not unique, nor a sign of inability
Correct the vision and it becomes tranquility

I have seen the world you cannot see
I have seen the gifts He has given thee
The pitfalls by His grace you stepped aside
The arrows His shield took, you found right to chide

The pounds you, yes, had to bear
The tons he bore you called air
I have seen the blessing given
Keep your faith, lest from Him you are driven

We live in a world of shadow and light
Our allegiance will show in what we delight
It is the opposite of the emperor's new clothes
God's clothes are real, not fake, as many suppose

The wise will see them and their purity
The foolish will not see, and chide with impunity

How do I better trust, as you say?
Yes, I know we shall meet some day
I feel abandoned and alone
So where has this trust gone?

Session Nine

You understand more than you know
I'll explain and to you show
By understanding, you avoid the gangrene of the soul
By this wisdom, you can reach the goal

Your condition may or may not change
You will see a dark for light exchange
The cure feels worse than the disease
Feeling is not the gauge, but how one sees (understands)

Your pain I see runs quite deep
Your answer base, will not keep
Your gauge isn't, does this cure me
But does the pain stop, that my key

Then you reject answers to do cure
And you want to accept others, even if manure
The pain you suffer is not lack of faith
To desire its removal isn't lack of faith

It isn't selfish to want it to go
Everybody would you know
It isn't selfish wanting human intimacy
It is a problem when it takes supremacy

Serenity prayer may help, but it needs reflection
The differences between reality and imagination
How much is imagined and what is fact?
Where to begin and with what tact?

Imaginations can see demons or angels
Which is which depends on our angles
We can imagine pain being great or small
Some can discount it much, or not at all

Temptation strikes, again I fail
At times it only takes a breeze, seldom a gale

I am doomed to sin no matter how I try
I fight on, and reason, I must get by
I have a constant sense of condemnation
With a sense of humiliation

Listen to me and you will see
I shall give you the door and the key
You have spoken, long to your ability
Listen to my picture of reality

It should offer you a hope
Give you tools so you can cope
I ask your kind attention
When done you may ask your question

For such loss as you have felt
People understand the hand you are dealt
To help relieve the pain you are feeling
To be anxious for nothing has no appealing

It is hard not to desire a cure for the pain
But it is now your ex-companion and your bane
It helps to grieve the loss and cry the tear
Grieve the loss, of love lost, a dream so dear

Pain is lowered if one is not desperate for something
Otherwise higher painful expectations it shall bring
Pressures from those friends near
Pressures from those you do not hold dear

Pressures within your own body
Pressures from the spiritual mind drive you batty
Pay attention to your self-speak
Examine the truth, is it hard, or is it weak

Remember to talk back and ask why
Examine it again, is it truth or a lie?
Step outside yourself and what you see
You see me talking to thee

If you talk about your problems in the 3rd person
It is easier to see the issues, and ask them a question
When you see and talk to yourself beware
Of your self-righteousness, and others you will have no care

In this one is right, in a wrong way even before God
Our own justification is not the way we should have trod
Our own right in justice we plead
If we push God's dismay we may succeed

In our pain then we reap bitterness an evil eye
In our pleasure we reap feelings or superiority, a high I
It matters not the class, rich or poor
Our religion or irreligious, negligence or a doer

Our will when thwarted, it feels pain
When one submits, to our will, our pleasure, our gain
Ask what is important and you will see
Do what is right, for others and for thee

An example will suffice
Smile at people, or pay the price
It will help their day and yours too
But if they don't, that is them not you

We are not asking you to walk on water
But do some small thing that does matter
Do it daily, in the mood or not
Work for ill or good is not forgot

Good will add to good inside
As bad to bad, which is your guide
You choose the action and attitudes to behold
To the blind, same, one is lead and the other gold

Walk the steps one at a time
The payoff isn't a dollar, but a dime
To go quickly, a rush is destined to fall
The little pays in time, interest adds a big haul

Self-speak you can do, even a bit
You can test, try the thought, prove it
You are able to act on your plan
Goals to reach, day, week, month, say "I can!"

Know you can ferret out the feelings you have
Know how they encourage you to behave
I can choose my attitude to that or this
I will see it this way, be burning or bliss

Not to escape stark reality
This is to keep the faith God has given me
He has faith in me to keep His word
I fall, but can walk again, and use His sword

He has given us His word, faith, love, and hope
Axioms for each other, through life's struggles we can cope
In the things you have been told
I have seen God's protection, even if cold

Even though He is feeling far away
He is with you, come what may
His hand is not always what you desire
Selective seeing we miss the blessing behind the fire

Certain seeds require fire in order to grow*
Seeds of faith need patience, work, His word applied to know
Time heals wounds, when medicine is applied
Allowed to fester become infected cannot be denied

You have the will I see to forgive
Freed from the binding chains and live
The shadows will haunt that is true
They need not control, or hinder you

*Serotinous cones need the intense heat of a fire to open, then
afterwards are able to spread their seeds and grow from the ashes
of the fire that burned before it.

Realize they are present and move on
They hold nothing; their message is a con
Not to justify "my being right"
That will make me self-righteous and uptight

Content with such as what I have got
Finding simple pleasures, in wonder, as a tot
Not childishness, but patient trust
God will provide; we work, pray, as we must

Journal and keep a log
It will help to dispel the fog
It will help to keep clarity of thought
Things, feelings, which are not as they ought

It keeps a history of progress done
It keeps perspective of battles lost and won
It sorts the feelings and questions that we ask
It helps us to focus on the task

It is not speed that counts here
But patient remembrance of our efforts and values we hold
dear
Remember the anchor that you have had through this
Consider, you may not be the problem you should not
dismiss

You have value; you have to live
Through pain alone, and put through a sieve
You had your dreams you feel you need to see
Working, options, time, others, this is meaningful to thee

The guiding light to the very end
His word a comfort, we read again, 'til he shall descend
By this doing, seeing, This He is present
In tears of joy and grief, our security is transcendent

We understand the discipline of the Lord
The warm fuzzies, the chastening, the good it does afford
Examine yourself and your past
Recognize what it is that you hold fast

This life you realize was a gift
You do not want to exist to drift
When in your hope in God you feel despair
When you feel beyond any hope of repair

Remember God created worlds from nothing
Now He gives a chance to help and co-make something
Your faith in God little as it may have been
Will grow when cultivated, much to the devil's chagrin

He cannot stop your trust or will
Do God's will, it is for Him you take a bitter pill
We work and cannot see the end result
Our faith in God, in the end, our blinders melt

The faith of Abraham, not for unbelievers, not him
But for those who are serious, and not on a whim
Just as he could not see, but we see it now
We cannot see, but other's will when we fulfill our vow

Our love is not a fancy sort of thing
But helps the need, and the blessings it will bring
As a patient of a doctor and medicine taken
We submit or do the good, trust and even in ach'in

This brings comfort in the end
Our health regained, we did mend
This we can give as God does according to our means
This is the relationship we have, by our spiritual genes

We can count on it; God is in control
Even when it appears most evil, a very heavy toll
God controls both times of either, why, how and when
In the end, it is for God's glory, who dares condemn

With this perspective we forge what we believed
Unbelievers call delusion, blindness, self-deceived
There isn't comfort in cynicism gone to seed
It will not fulfill any real human need

You have experienced this and other emotions of a kind
You can judge, examine them in their mind
Let us now ask and answer no more why I want to die
Let us now no more believe the self-speak that does lie

Let us ask now and answer why I want to live
Let us sing self-speak, why I will survive
Things I plan and pursue come what may
My motivation to try from day to day

Ahh, the dreams, or nightmares of the mind
How much is ours, or theirs, and which will we bind?
Consider, meditate, think, then speak
What is thy heart, now, the choice of the meek?

A long-winded therapist thou art today

No more so than another I dare say

You expect much to break it down to basic element
Me to paraphrase? I am not eloquent
The Bible is the "answer key"
That is what many say to me

The answer to life's questions
There is no index on my inspections
Think on the nobility of the chivalry
Think on the noble battles against all odds victory

You ask me to create the words that don't exist
Create the images we see from life's foggy mist
In a humble way, my words to express
Eternal truth to impress, or make a mess

The universe existence, the fabric of God's thought
Woven thread of words of light, as God taught
Pictures on a child's security blanket, of faith, hope and love
We become His blood relative* heeding wisdom from above
(*When we obey the gospel of Jesus Christ)

The master of the universe wants a life shared with me
I am not to comprehend it; only relate and let it be
Do the things He asks of me in loving duty, as I am able
When all is done, He will then grant me a place at His table

Commend the soul to the loving God our Creator
I surrender to His will, my salvation's maker
Hear this prayer I make
I pray the Lord, He shall take

Grant me eyes that shall see
The things I need to do for thee
Grant me a mind to understand
The Truth you have, to do and to comprehend

Grant me hands strengthened of thee
To do Thy will, you give to me
Grant me courage for my feet
To go fight on even if I see defeat

Grant me a tongue for words well seasoned
Be they sweet, or salt, be it well said and reasoned
Grant me an ear to hear
To listen to those in despair and fear

Grant that I may surrender to thy will indeed
Grant what I offer is acceptable service following your lead
You have given faith in thee
By Christ's sacrifice for me

You have given me blessings in your love
By seeing, trusting your providential hand from above
You have given me hope that in the future end
I'll be enveloped in the promised love when you descend

In Jesus's name I pray this prayer
A prayer and trust that thou shalt hear
Alas, the pain it comes and goes and comes again
The pain I feel, and see the shadows are profane

I tire of this again and again and again
It is hard to throw aside this painful binding chain

The cross is also painful to bear
Think of Christ and He'll be there
It is hard to discern which pains are which
Lest we cast aside the wrong one, thinking we are rich

Remember the words that thou hast said
Find a patient friend, of God, one with a level head
To do the trust as you have said, to me as you had
Trust the God as you work to do the good in spite of the bad

The Bible is a book of answers, yes
It answers the questions from life's mess
It is not the answer and it is done
It is here the answer; your choice has begun

It isn't just that here is a book to believe however dim
This is the man from the book; do you believe in Him?
He has a teaching to set you free
The road you walk, for self or He?

Remember the road is not one of speed
But love and loyalty to God and His creed
Do not worry what you haven't got
Use what is in your hand; see that it doesn't rot

Pain doesn't separate you from God on high
As you said, you shall then be with Him when you die
Concentrate as I may say
Not on the dark alone, but in the day

We know why it is that you want to die
Try to turn your thoughts, I want to live, says I
Why do I want to live?
The reason is there and there to give

This reason gives hope to one and every soul
Think on this, pain can be used by Jesus, to make you whole

They sound like high words you have there

So you say, you have said them, are they air?

No, they are not, I know they are true
They are heavy, either coming from me or you
I am sorry it was what I had felt
I repent of that my heart does melt

Day to day, I will find my song
Day to day, as I trudge along
I want to live; that is true
If I don't, I am through

I want to live it is hard
Evil sings too like a bard
I must disregard his siren song
It hurts my heart to say no for so long

To understand the world God made
To understand what is indeed His aide
I will take steps slow and sure
Know His ways, even if I am unclear

I will ever pray to God
Until at last I rest below the sod
Until that time I want to live and breathe
Maybe I can show someone, so they believe

Lord grant me this strength so I can cope
I can help someone else to hold on to the rope
Help me to see what is a threat and what is not
Help me to see what it is that I have got

Forgive the rambling of the anguishness of the heart
It is then I look to you, and say, "How great thou art"

I want to live and finally this I'll do
Because I want you to know, I do trust you

I want to live for God above
For I have seen His care and love
I can tell why I want to live
When I die, My life I wish to give

Not the works that I have done
But to thank Him, because of what I've become
It is a gift life to me He brought
So I'll become what He has taught

God gave life, a gift to you
This is as some have said it is true
What you do is a gift returned to the Lord
The Lord will return good on His word

So let me strive to struggle on
We've nothing to lose, but Hell, and for Heaven we long
That is why I will strive for life
Even in the midst of this strife

I desire to live, and that is why
Deep down I do not want to die
I tire of trying to live, so I desire to die
I tire of dying, so I must again live and try

I have a conviction of faith to keep and give
A faith in God, that is why, for him, I want to live
That is why I fight the wish to die
Help me Lord, save me from this I cry

It is hard to fight the pain, despair, to God to give
Deeper down, work for a gift to God, for that I want to live.

Section II

Why I Want to Live

Introduction

In the previous section, I concluded with, "I want to live." Section II takes up where section I left off. The pain and residual issues and troubles that come with that may forever be with me, as a haunting ghost. The struggles continue even after choices are made. As the battles are fought, the "Therapist" tries to point out that you will get better at it, even if they do haunt you through life. There are recurring battles and memories that haunt the patient and myself. As the therapist, at first, I was just giving advice to help, realizing that here was a person who could help with their walk with Christ. Thus, the therapist wants to keep company with such a person with such convictions.

The description I have tried to describe is one of conviction of faith in the providence of God. One part is in knowing who God is and that we can trust Him. The second part is in our being faithful to what He has said, that shows God we can trust Him. This is not an effort of merit. This is an honest effort that I know who I am, I know who you are, and we both know what is and what is here, so help me to be what you (God) have created me to be. There are some poems that are references to a line or two within this long dialogue. These are in another collection of poems I am working on.

In having read the words of both, I hope I can live up to what it is I have written. I hope to have upheld God's word, as it is suppose to be. Nothing written here is really new; the concepts are all in scripture, principles and ideals. May this be for His glory. I still have a ways to go.

The answer to the prayer at the end of the session was answered. In November 2004, the answer came when a fellow Christian showed me a book, *Marriage and Divorce*, by John L. Edwards. This book showed an understanding of scripture I had not had before. It indicated I could get married again.

As I have reached one conclusion, I have found that there are others who would roundly condemn me. Lord, grant that I may only rule where you rule and leave out where you have not. Help me, Lord, to live again up to what I have written. The default of what it means is hard. It is a broken world as many have said. I have come to conclude that there are more ways to break the word where He has not "ruled." This too is a sin. Faith in what is a sin is not right; it will not save. There is the sin in immorality and ignoring God's word. There is the imposing of an interpretation of God's word on others where God has not ruled. Wisdom should tell us what is what. We should be able to tell the difference between the love of the Truth, and what we take for the "Truth."

This is hard on many issues, by the issue of divorce and remarriage, or another. As before, if one is depressed, get help!

To God be the glory,

B. L. Phipps

Session Ten

When I review where I came
I can see how I was lame
I was spinning, dizzy in a cold bottomless pit
There was no solace found in it

Then as I talked, examined the soul
Discerned the causes, the pain, wrote my goal
I kept falling but the spin did not stop
I still felt poorly, falling long from the top

Then as I saw through the pain in its mirage
I struggled to gain understanding of the collage
I saw the ways and means to bind the wounds
The descent slowed, fears deflated like balloons

The descent came to a painful stop
I re-assessed myself, is what I got
The throbbing pain comes and goes
Always there, increases with fears and woes

But now clinging to the pit's side
I begin to climb, grateful, yet I hadn't died
The way is long, painful and steep
There is a long way before I sleep

Now the tools for climbing and healing
Tools to adjust when emotions send me reeling
Tools to heal, understand, and plan ahead
Use them, hard and heavy, follow directions as you have read

Weights that burden me
The arrows of regret won't let me be
The pain of past, the hard future ahead
It is overwhelming; I long, wish I were dead

The shame, the brand, the shaming mark
I still sense I am climbing in the dark

The vision still of my life's gift to the Lord
What can I do, I have nothing I see I can afford
I pray the Lord to help me; there is no peace
I long for death that will bring release

The price runs high, more than I've got
I've nothing to pay; my assets are shot
I pray the Lord, help me; there is no peace
Where is the plan that will bring release?

Rites of passage, tests of pain through the fight
Are not restricted to adulthood of secret societies of night
Rites of passage through tragedies of life
Loss of family, property, work, and divorce, husband or wife

Dealing with emotions that arise, shadows that appear alive
Bitterness or in hate one sinks, or forgive, you swim and survive
Trust the compass setting you have set
Ignore the feelings and threatening monsters you have met

Take one step, one day, as you know is true
Pray for God; it depends on him, work of faith depends on you
Aware of the emotions and their organization
Aware of how they are of your own creation

Assumed size and dimension and strength and threat
You so much give them what power that they get
Figure what is true and what is not
Discern the threat, the true form and what it's got.

The pain hurts, no denying its existence
But, must you by fear give the pain assistance?
You have the dream I want to live
Upon this hill you will die, not for a lie

The fight is yours and fight again and again and again
Plan, know illusion, real and not, future, what the past has been
Be true to the dreams and not fear the bitterness and pain
The fight you win, the victory is not for you, but God's gain

It has been said those who fail to learn from past mistakes
Repeat them in the future, and close improvements' gates
This is true of any nation, race, and tongue
True of people whether grouped, or just one

Discerning what is an error and what is not
Not just morals, but personal growth, a mental knot
I move as it were in water, I cannot run
I move in a maze, every day, I've just begun

A force field around what I want to do
If I work, it pains me to be true
There is no progress, benchmarks to see
Only a troubling paradox, I'm adrift at sea

It pains me, not to work what I want
It pains me more to make the effort so I recant
There is no win
So I don't begin

The dark emotions do return
With a vengeance they do burn
It's all I can do to keep them at bay
They are nameless, a mysterious they

Ahhh, the shadows of the night
Illusions, inciting fear, a paralyzing plight
The shadows' illusions that they have mass
A reality, we touch, a reality of mind a different class

Are you convinced your fear is real?
What is fear? Truth will reveal
Your belief adds flesh to the skeleton
Your imagination gives life to this demon

You are in water as you say
But our beliefs intensify the "they"
By our thoughts the water boils or is as ice
When people say yes, or no, or when things are nice

Everyone moves as slow in the water of life
Those who do well can swim in the strife
What I am trying to do with you
Teach you to swim the strokes that will get you through

Now you have come to learn to tread the water
Now you have learned to float, that does matter
When you came, you were drowning
The sea of emotion was overwhelming

Now to learn to swim again
You will learn better than you did back then
You have to learn to swim with your malady
Learn to swim as in a new reality

The senses are the same
With practice, swim as before the event came
So now, again, learn the stroke
Relearn application of Him who spoke

A sinful, tempting false assessment I am not
It is on what you are, what you have got
A graceless judgment of the standard outside of self
Such a standard would put us all on the shelf

The beginning moves you try in pain
This practice you think is hard, a bane
It is by small things as said before
It will enable you to do more

The waves will return time and again
These storms can be withstood, future, as well as then
Understand the vision of your eyes
What's their value, and you can realize

The reality and world of the shadows you fear
Will fade, no terror, though they be "near"
They will not your future determine
They will burn; they are vermin

Let God's evaluation be your test
Let His voice, admonish and give you rest
Do not try to command the water
Command not the current, it doesn't matter

They are not the elements of your control
The waters that are yours are in your soul
They can boil or be as ice
They can be churning or quiet and nice

They are yours despite the sea without
They are yours in solitude, or when others shout
Remember time too is at God's command
Yours to do, if you don't finish, God will understand

Calm yourself, work as you can
God's in charge, the great I AM
The choice is yours on which to act
For good or ill, think of them, choose carefully how you will
react

Comforting, so I thought
Teach me as I ought
How can I know this confidence isn't self-deception?
How can I know I am going in the right direction?

Many have found "peace" of which you speak
But only to be found to miss what they seek
The peace I want is not there
Where it is suppose to be, a void without air

Excellent question that you ask
I will answer, but yours the task
Contentment such as what you own
But when you covet, you have anxieties and moan

This creates dissention within
A division of values, of the soul, a sin
This can be with goals and who we are
When reality isn't what we want, it is balance that we bar

This ideal is our own we can create
If it isn't God's, it is ours, and thus we desecrate
We can do God's will as He has said
We can do as he has led

The self-deception becomes apparent
When we take something of God's by any percent
If we presume on His grace
That offense we can't erase

If we humbly try to obey
Do His will along life's way
He will judge who is what
The faithful servant and the mutt

Sorry, I digress to your question
Honesty and truth, the stars for your direction
Self-deception will rationalize the falsehood to a truth
The honest will admit the wrong, change from the uncouth

Study God's word and yourself in reflection
Let truth, not feelings, guide your action's direction
The peace you want, let us examine
Is it with God, the world, and the mammon?

If it is with the world
If achieved, your soul is imperiled
If it is with God, a worthy goal
God will help you and make you whole

While you fight for this peace
Realize the binding and release
You cannot try to keep the world and its values
It will conflict with you and you must pay its dues

Flee to God and the devil will follow
Creating problems, paradoxes, and lies to the bones' marrow
Regret the past, a normal thing
Press on to the truth and heed its ring

The pains we carry and cares of the past
When to Jesus we come at last
Tribulation comes with woes
Satan tries deception with new lows

Pains will come, but cannot harm our tie to the Lord
We feel it true, the hurt, the cutting sword
The pain's illusion is not the pain
But that it separates we have no gain

Sometimes it is wrong to feel no pain, creating apathy
We then lose our sense to feel empathy
Pain tells us something is wrong
It makes a distance for what we long

Our mind by our values and standards the error
It makes people villains, or people of valor
Take care lest you think yourself righteous in your ways
Be humble, for it is God who numbers our days

Truth exists in an objective form
It isn't always in you or the public norm
God's standard will always ring true
Examine then the number of perspectives too

Your eyes and what you see
Your standard to be true to thee
Would you want to be receiving what you give?
Never mind what others do as you live

God's eyes and what He does see
What does God see of thee?
What does your neighbor see?
What you speak, and do, and be?

High words of wisdom do I hear
I wish my heart were closer and more near
My heart has missed some tenor of your word
I've only caught half of what I've heard

I am sorry I digress
I shall apply it to your stress
Realize you can still move, walk, yes you can
You have a compass; you need not wander, like a lost lamb

Do you fear because it isn't perfect now?
Unless you can, you refuse to bow
As said before, do what you can
You can move and live as to your plan

It need not be perfect, but well enough, if best
That being true, it will pass the test

So you say so easily to me in this house
My best wasn't good enough from my spouse

Forgive how cruel this may sound
Was your spouse your standard from the sky to ground?
The assessments of which I speak
They are yours, the valley and mountain peak

It is tragic, yes, if it isn't shared
But it is still yours, you have dared
Know your faith, your spouse's rejection of you
It isn't God's rejection, repent, He will see you through

There may be pain for a time
It must not control you, even if you are inclined
Be sure your assumptions are real
It is to reason I appeal

Not emotions, for they are prone to err
Emotions' reasons assume facts that aren't there
It is these interpretations I would have you examine
Test the facts are they true, carefully determine

Thus will come a reality from which to walk
Thus you can move, work, live truth, fear not, nor balk
Your spouse is powerless though may try to inflict harm
Beware, know the truth, for falsehood will try to work its
charm

Suspicion can cause you to err
If you act on these fears, you become trouble's heir
The fears are not of people only
They may be simple, cars, computers, eating baloney

Test the confidence carefully of what you know
Is that true or false, by it you grow
Contrast these as you live each day
You will see a mastery that will pay

You will gain a sense of control
Because you have fueled your self-esteem with new petrol
Move on these newfound fuels
Maintain the engine, its value is above jewels

Is this presumption that I learn?
If it is, a Hell I do earn

There is presumption that is true
Obedience and humility remove it from you
Bow the knee to God above
Obey and move within His love

Plan and move and do what you enjoy
If it is not a sin, that work your mind and body you employ
There is no crime in this what you do
Many won't care, some not like, just concern yourself with
you

This isn't selfishness in this case we talk
This is what we offer in life as we walk
The selfishness of what you worry
Are those who take, from giving as they hurry

If others refuse what you offer
It isn't a reflection on what you proffer
Be at your best and if they refuse
It is not anything; there is no abuse

Live for the voice of God who speaks
He looks for those, who for Him seeks
His praise is what you need to be alive
Do His will and you will survive

Serve His concerns here on earth
With your talents, His salvation will be your birth
Confidence, awareness of God and His creation
Pray, watch, you find peace even in affliction

Examples of money we take for what we do
We believe their word and money through and through
Consider when we ask for the time
Are we regarded, and believe their words, or take it as a crime

When we ask for the food we eat
Do we take it as poison or a treat?
If these words of people we respect and believed
Will not God give us our need, and our need relieved?

If others refuse their task on earth and refuse His cue
God will consider it of them, not you
So believe the Lord and His work to do
In your ability to work and express your "you"

For His glory as creator of the universe
To claim our space and right is perverse
In humility, do, you have and know
Your confidence in Him will grow

Take God then at His word then as He said
He will fulfill His word, as He has written, and you have read

I will write what must be
I will test the words of thee
I will find the facts both true and false
I will embrace the truth, the lie repulse

Allow the time to reflect on your words and thoughts
I will attempt to record and do the oughts

I will not fear the failure that may come
I will, in hope, finish the course within and out what may become
           (pause)
But what of the pain that will return
The pain regardless, the fuel it does burn
The loneliness, sex or failure or other
It is strong and self-esteem it does smother

Pains will come; pains will go
Pleasures will come and pleasures will go
They are weather of life
As are success and strife

We strive to work as well as we can
Regardless of challenges and problems arise despite our plan

What you say sounds well and good
Just do the things, as I should
But the pains that haunt and return
The things that make the soul doth burn

What of the shame that lies within
What of my unknown crimes and sin
The regrets of wrongs I've done
Are we not the product of the past, I'm undone

What you say is true to a point
Your destiny is yours; it is quaint
If your path should take a bad turn or two or three
You can change it, only you, not others, God, me

God has determined much; that is true
But your heeding, what you do, it is up to you
These ghosts can haunt you if you let them though
These things of the past, even comfortable pain, let it go

A new world, new pains 'tis true
But new beginnings for a happier you
It will mean a bit of effort to find what works
A bit of discomfort and planning though the quirks

Repeat a thing till you get it right
Fear not mistakes or it will be your plight
Perfection is everything; certainly is a worthy goal
But when it becomes a hindrance, it trips up the soul

That perfect is the composition of the soul
That bears the foibles of life, a rut or a hole
We are not to judge by the standards this life has to offer
But more of what we become of ourselves to God we proffer

The soul's condition is what is important to Him
To disregard His word is most grim
But for now, realize as you believe and grow
Nothing can separate you from God's love, you know

As you walk on, what you do for Him
Kindness to others, enemies, shine your light, even if you
think dim
It may be the only light others see
He is your encouragement He is your praise, not the world, or
me

High-sounding words I must say
Stay true to God come what may
The encouragement of others helps too
Even if it does, I hope, come from you

That too is a part of this light show
To be a true light, not a performance glitter and go
I will again consider these words of yours
Be not surprised if I return full of bumps and sores

Despite the words you say
The pain continues day to day
The work helps; this is true
But this pain still exists mocking me, you

It says I will stay and that is that
It comes inside and hangs its hat
What can be done to stem the painful tide?
These waves of acid emotion I can't abide

I have a hope the pain will end
I have a hope I'll have a friend
I have a hope I can still cope
I have a hope I'll not swing on a rope

Where do I get self-confidence, I confess
When my life feels such a mess
I don't believe what my enemies say of me
It is not true what they say of thee

It is hard to believe the words of grace
It is hard to look at myself, mirror and soul, face to face
My life is no longer the light it was again
No longer the life it might have been

The iron fence God's known will
But jump the fence or not I'll feel ill
I am paralyzed; I feel as wood
I am alive, but can't move as I should

This fear controls the fiber of my being
How to fight it and succeed, oh victory I long to sing

Do you know what you fear?
What is threatened that you hold dear?

My security is held and bound
Others can see this; my spouse holds the ground
They can hurt me, burn me so I cringe
I've been hit, I move, to prevent the singe

Forgive while I speak to thee
But it is you who holds your key
Despite how low one may be made to sink
It is you who determines what you think

Many can determine the outward affliction
But it is you who say, this is my attitude and action
Even if a world destroyed
Your attitude, your choice they can't avoid

My choices hurt when wrong 'tis true
Think, I can change; I'm not responsible for the choices of
you
I can repent of what I have done
I can begin, plan and have it begun

Do not try to recapture, resurrect the past
For starters, such an effort will not last
When we try to resurrect the dead
We may find demons that surround our bed

They won't be angels, nor heaven, as we want
It will be sick, lacking, a broken empty font
Instead build a new world
A new land for the flag unfurled

Your spouse can't launch an attack here
For starters, you no longer need to fear
As this final chapter of this event is written
You remember the feelings, origin, with what you were
smitten

Rebuild the dream on solid ground
Using the concrete skill, the foundation can be found
This work brings healing to the broken bone
As you plan it heals, dreams now made of heart to stone

To use the principles of which you speak
To hold them all I would seek

Are you sure the pain is all you are afraid?
Many fall short from another, thereby a block to aid
The work itself many shun
They say I do not want to toil in the hot sun

They say, I have no wish to work at night
I haven't the strength from the day, then my work site

Your point is well made
The dream won't live unless you've paid
I'll test the fears, large and small
I'll pursue them even if I have to crawl

I'll beat this thing, this heavy thought
I'll get behind and lift the ought
I'll put it in its place
By that strength to move by His grace

Failure is counted by lack of strength or will
Success is done by drill, drill, drill
What of the past failure I've suffered (the failed marriage)
By some actions or words I uttered

That success and failure depends on two
You both either succeed, or you both are through
If one attempt isn't your cup of tea
Try a different drink or recipe*

*This trying, ways to make marriage work, not simply by divorce
and another marriage!

You will find another calling to your ear
One where you will pursue and will not fear
Realize the confines written by the Lord of all
Within these limits, you will find your work, your call

Ah, the vision before mine eye
Always beckoning so I will try
A mirage I can understand
Even a law's command

What you say is a show of faith
Obey, thus, do what the Lord doth saith
The feelings are at odds with each other
Emotions and knowledge are lost to one another

I have lost the ability to relate
To peoples, things, goals, values, and my fate
My identity, a stranger, yet one I once knew
I do the things I need, hoping for a clue

I have my history, I remember, regret what was before
Learn from the re-mistakes from my foundation, my being's core
In order to rebuild the identity is most difficult to do
The plans are lost, how can I rebuild anew?

I know some things that I have and keep
But the way is hard, narrow trials, mountains steep
The map or computer's plan, lost, either example will apply
Find the compass, reboot the computer, anything says I

Where do I find the landmarks, or syntax relief?
The stars, stone marks, my journal, a manual of my belief?
There are problems of power not physical or mental
Where is the power to move the blocks, firm but gentle

Your self-doubt has gone extreme
I will tell you what I mean
You have your past in mind, for you have told me
You say, "I can relate it all to thee"

To reboot the system, a syntax error
A manual, to correct and avoid the terror
You have maintained the ties and healthy ways
Now you need to move, do the simple things these next days

Elementary I know, this will sound
But make a list,* do them and your identity will be found
Not my active paper definition to be read
But by your emotion to see by your own deed

Do your values on your list each day
Your plans do them as well as you can, despite delay

If interrupted, all is not lost to the plan
Retry your work, record the deeds, you will see you can
By doing these things, the blanks in your life will fill
By doing these things, the efforts will pay the bill

So can you tell me again, I hope I don't offend
What is your guiding star, my friend?

My guiding star? Why I want to live?

Assuredly, that is the answer I hope you'll give

My guiding star of what drives my will
Is the hope, by my work, other's life I can fill
But my work and what I say
I'll be true come what may

To find the strength through proper nutrition
I'll not starve my neglect to achieve my soul's proper ambition
I'll be patient and work on my therapy each day
I'll do what I cannot fear and do I pray

*This list is a list of things that the patient considers worthwhile
and interesting.

A proper diet of the mind and mental filter
Will keep me healthy and from getting out of kilter
To exercise and think and discern
This to do, to do and learn

To work focused, study to be
What God created, a gift, from me to Thee
By relying on the compass* that I've got so far
It is counted true, precious as the guiding star

Being true to myself I'll carry on
I've been finding some strength and some fun
The shadows still threaten substance I feel
Their chill, their jaws; hoping I'll run and reel

I digress; my feelings are weak kneed
How to strengthen them is what I need
The ghosts of my regret
Are cause of much anxiety and fret

I cannot seem to let them go
Indeed, when I cut, I find they grow
The memory of the past continues on
For its solution to the problems, I do long

Regrets feast upon, "If only I had done"
Can you be sure the ending, if different, would be more fun?
A hundred choices and changes we can make
Which can we be sure of and which to take?

We cannot take responsibility for what others choose to do
The best we can do, is try to know then see it through

Mistakes that haunt us every day
That is a heavy price to pay
Either by what we have done
Or done to us, we've lost, not won

*Compass is the Bible to discern the wrong or rightness of the
options offered when our desires might be one direction or
another.

How to deal with this cancerous pain
This ghost is an unending bane
The repair I do as I can
Fulfill the duties, and do the plan

But I am not happy with my life
There is a fault line; it cuts like a knife
It goes beyond the bone marrow
It threatens how I feel and see tomorrow

I have no desire to continue, in woe is me
I have no desire for my self-pity
I want to break free of its iron grip, this fist
Nothing brings happiness, lost direction in life's foggy mist

Then we apply pressure to the wrist

What is it that you suggest?
This is most difficult to understand and apply the test

What causes pain in our physical body?
An invader causing a malady
Nerves let us know of the invasion
Research, MO, tell us the occasion

The pain of the soul, pain of perception
By the value system, determines stimuli's reception
The hurt is felt, imagined or real
Our choice is what action; by what authority we place our seal

By our choice, right or wrong, splitting hairs with a knife
The power we give it, is the power it has in our life
Does this match the reality that we see?
That too is a choice, I submit to thee

Changing is always harder than status quo
Depending on the change, depends on amount of woe
This depends on your worldview
What does it say about the world to you?

Is it true or is it not?
Who is it that says what you've got?

O.K. We can talk about change
What are the benchmarks, what is their range?
Why are they there is one task?
What should they be? Another question I do ask

There are benchmarks, as you say
They have a price, dues to pay
But not in money in the bank or on credit
But by action, attitude, or our action to it

The habits to do and watch to adopt
These start with little choices that we opt

What to do when the desire to die comes, it returns
The Bible readings offers no hope, the help, it burns
There are no promises for the Christian here
All my hopes leave, they disappear

My appeals to God seem small, faint and weak
I am of no account, my appeals, my arguments they leak
All men earn more where I attend
My contribution to do, I cannot amend

My skills to work are only fair
There are many who exceed me there
My ambition in business, is that I am of no account
If I complain, I am a whiner, I feel they'll shout

They say I am not making the most of my talent
I feel I see no options, or express what I meant
I fear being stabbed in the back, thorns in the side
Lest my sin dirty them, none to turn to and with me abide

I have lost my self-esteem, you hear
I once again of my spouse, I live in fear
I live in terror of an angry God, Hell I await
The pain remains and leaves not my gate

An ever-present companion that weighs down my thought
Shackles the mind, to what I know I ought

On one level the threat is real
But I want to suggest first another appeal

Does God judge us by our wealth?
Does this gauge our spiritual health?
Does God judge us by what we see we give?
Is it on that basis we are allowed to live?

Does God judge us by our status in the world?
Is that really the standard by His welcome or that we are
hurled?

Does God judge us by what we might have or could do?
Or by what is ours, we have, what I do for Him, and you?
Does God judge us by ambition and its result?
Is that the how and why He judges the salt?

God judges us by what we do with what we have
Do our best, obey Him, he has promised this is a salve
Your spouse may take your property and dollar
But your spouse can't take what you believe above the collar

Your spouse cannot change your status before the Lord
It is He, not your spouse, who holds the sword
Now the desire to die is tied to pain
What is that to, this binding chain?

They seem tied to rejection
An amplified dejection
I thought I had it licked
Now I feel I have been tricked

My relief and hope have been removed
There is no peace; I'm disapproved

The spouse's continued rejection hurts, no question
But there may be problem with perception
That pain is not God's rejection of you
They are different, is this not true?

Upon what do you base God's rejection?
You repented, changed your direction
What is threatened in your offer to the Lord?

I may be required to give what I cannot afford

I fear my spouse may hinder and take more away
What fear I earn it is to the spouse I must pay
I hate myself for my faults
I can't improve or get better results

I have not resources to stop the spouse's purposes on me
I have not resources to earn more, which might be a key
If I did earn more by some twist of fate
The spouse would ask for more even more to date

This too hangs heavy on the mind and heart
If I could, fine, I can't, so I can't start

I feel I have disowned the faith I had
No money, support, so I've been bad
Thus salvation's hopes are waning
I fear God's face, his is disdaining

You are confusing the rejections you are feeling
There are two, to your reason I am appealing
The spouse's rejection does not affect your salvation
God does not base this on your spouse's deviation

You tried your best with what you knew
That is all God asks of you
Salvation is based on your faithfulness to God and what He said
The number of troubles is nothing, even being dead

Although pain exists and the threats you see
They again have bearing on how God sees thee
Pleasures exist too, and remember this well
They too have a being to God and with Him to dwell

Your response to the circumstance does make the difference
By your actions, they determine your true frame of reference

My eyesight on this is poor
Death still beckons and there is the door
When it is attention I want and warmth and security
Now these things in my life are a rarity

Your attention is grieving on a lost event
Remarriage, forbidden, divorce, the fabric of life is rent

I always desired marriage, now a dream gone bad
It became a nightmare, how tragic, how sad

Are you sure it was a total loss, some 18 years?
It will take time, but you can overcome the fears

Ahh, the other issues from the divorce
Identity lost, a lost resource
The self-hate and recrimination
Within the loss of my salvation

The loss of ability to concentrate
You say it will come, if I work and wait
So what is the cure, the therapy
Can half a mind work, if it puts me in jeopardy?

I have dreamt what happens in suicide
I get attention, warmth, I get taken inside

It is true of which you speak
It is not lasting for what you seek
You get these things; that is true
But it forces a relationship that isn't you

But to battle what you are up against
Hope must be restored, the threats chained and fenced

How do you rebuild what was lost
Resources gone, count the cost
There is nothing left to build on a destroyed foundation

Are they really? Remember creation

Resources are gone, to what do you refer, options you cannot see?
They are there in truth for thee
Your dreams haven't bit the dust
You still have them; they don't rust

Fallen true from their place of glory
Your faith in them may tell another story
There are people who can assist
Believe me they do exist

What you have told me
I will reiterate to thee
Your self-speak if you listen to your talk
It is will, or can keep you from your walk

"This can't go on, no hope of being married
"I hate this, I feel I must die and be buried
"End the pain, there is no peace
"I desire forbidden romance, marriage release

"I can't seem to function without a wife
"So I can't function throughout life"
The self-speak goes round and round
To break the cycle, a solution must be found

The pat answers are hard to apply
Many plea, tell me, what am I?
No mechanisms in place to move ahead
Blind to options, many would rather just be dead

Fear of criticisms and harsh replies
Even a remark hurts more than most realize
Many sentences without compassion
There are emotions in addition to the reason

I can't concentrate, with this pain of mine
The sadness is too great; all I do is pine
Condemned I feel for not doing what others say
Their advice misses, their suggestions miss, but I must pay

You know what I say
From the past to this day.

Session Twelve

As I have said before
Is this self-speak true or folklore?
Test the words to see if they are true
Are these things true, what they say of you?

Do you set yourself up to fail?
See I am nothing, I can, then wail
That isn't the life you really want
No life is built in saying, I can't

Our mental and emotional blocks may shield from the pain
They also shield us from what we might gain
A prayer, Lord help me to know what is mine and what I got
Help me to know what is my lot

Grant me eyes and mind to see
What the difference is, so I grow closer to thee
If there are options you can't abide
Why not write it out, or have you tried?

Is there more than one solution?
Are there problems in it, creating the pollution?
Know what is real or imagined deprivations
Things are hard enough without demonized imaginations

What truly made you happy in the past?
Those qualities in what you do will create happiness at last

What you say is what I will try to do
What will get me past the pain and get me through?

The pain you feel is a gift to thee
It tells you something is wrong with me
But it doesn't say what the cure ought to be
Some symptoms do provide clues to the key

But other pains are more vague, unknown
They exist; we feel them and are alone
We can reflect and ask what it is, and not
That gives us clues to what we've got

There are certain things to realize, solution's role
Solutions of the body will not help the pain of the soul
Drink will not help an empty guilt-ridden heart
That is an example from the start

There are other things I could use and say
But one example is enough, if I may
Guilt over temptation and some other things brings grief
A suggestion isn't a sin; understanding thus can bring relief

Use it rather as a means, as a point to ponder
For a while, O.K. but dangerous to go much yonder
For example it is not a sin to desire food
But to eat, eat, eat, often it is so rude

Guilt about an event beyond your control?
Assess what was my part, my effort, an honest goal
Let us determine lasting values beyond the grave
They'll bring to you, once adhered to, will surely save

Being desperate for this world's zest?
Will bring certain pain and little rest
Be desperate for nothing; learn to say no to desire
Desire is one thing, as need to want, as warm is to fire

Pains will change their character and label
Unless you realize this, you'll remain unstable
To mislabel the pain, the solution will not be a cure
You are still stuck with the pain, and again must endure

As pains come and pains go
Out lot is painful here below
Doing what's important and sharing pain can soothe
There is a collective strength; its use can prove

Make certain the pain within doesn't turn to bitterness
The pain changes, too, to a blind self-righteousness
The pain you had at first was rejection
Then it changed to a pain of isolation

It is changing again to loss and regret
It has been changing as we've talked and met
The feelings have changed emphasis from time to time
Be assured from this pit, we can help you climb

Our suffering can be for others' sins on us, deliberate or
candid
Other suffering can be our sins that we did
Being a Christian, there are struggles without and within
Without are efforts to hold the path, within, deny the walk
therein

All to get you to compromise your life and Christ
To water it down, rob his doctrine, for yourself, what a heist

I agree and experience what you have observed me to say
But on either score, there is a price to pay
The world becomes a harsh and bitter place
When once one experiences cold water in the face

It is hard to remove the chill from the bone
There is no warm place to call my own
When all warm sources cease, warmth becomes the goal
Another pain, warmth at all cost, will cost the soul

But I cannot sacrifice that warmth for eternity
My Lord, and His grace, mean more than that to me

Detachment of ownership of what this world esteems
By this view, the pain can be reduced it seems
This world is only a trust from the Lord
It is truly a mistake to try to hoard

All things of this world are only an incidental
It is our treatment of this trust that is quintessential
But consider yourself only His employee
Entrusted with His goods to thee

Note again, the goods are not all He owns
He owns you for work in the heavens, so you He hones
Battles between worldly and Godly sorrow we are beset
Pain, comes in fighting with choices, and feelings we may
regret

Choose which side you will take
Both have pain, and one's a mistake

The world offers solutions to this pain
The devil hopes to ensnare it is his feign
With the worldly solution, pain goes away indeed
But by doing so, we deny God's creed

God offers solutions to and for the soul
As has been said, it makes you whole
So when the pains without, invade your life
They do not offer even half the strife

The pains within that cause much concern
Will and can go away with what we can learn
Your self-esteem may fight your view of reality
Expectations of yourself, if not correct, can cause a malady

For too much or too little creates a hurt
By such a view, we miss things, for which we are not alert
Pain can confuse our values, discernment, lack of strength
and will
Conflict in values may need understanding, which takes skill

To understand the context of living in this life
Like knowledge, sharp blades, cuts benefit or bleeds from the
knife
Then we wonder what and how we did the wrong
Handling of life, like a knife, needing practice to be good and
strong

Where do I gain this strength, and eyes and mind to see
Understanding and my will to do and find the right key?
Many claim to have such keys
Which are right? The wrong ones will be as bees

In the end that is true
Before that happens, one believes it is in you

In being detached, is not losing self
You are not putting your values on the shelf
Being spiritual is being aware of life and the senses
Being aware of others, empathy lowers defenses

We can become aware of our place in creation
We work with what is His, according to His operation
It is not detachment of our reason, intellect and logic
Mysterious? True, but abandonment of reason is tragic

How do I then grasp the spirit of which you speak?
How do I gain this? And become among the meek

Awareness of life in the context of life's actions
What is permitted and not, for many this causes factions
The whole picture creates an understanding that speaks to all
But not to those who wish to carry the ball

It is not theirs to carry or gain the glory
It is God's game, His rules, and His story
The world's ideas for problems and their solution
Are many more times, in God's eyes, pollution

So when you try to grapple with your painful war
Are your solutions the problem, creating pain, not less, but more?
Mean it or not the emotions and impulses of the ignorant heart
It creates more confusion, and pain it doesn't have to impart

Discern, ask why
Is it real or imagined, understand, I must try
Look outside in, watch and inside out
Discern the pain and what it's all about

All this thought and consideration
It is hard and it's enumeration
The feelings come and feelings go
They create pain with their ebb and flow

When on the feelings I have a grip
They slip through and out of it
The feelings of suicide come and return
Again I feel the heat and I do burn

They come on like an adrenaline rush.
They force action, now feelings I can't hush
The emotional fighting to do what's right
To still the flame, and destruction takes a fight

I desire a harmony within at least and at last
But none comes, I pray and fast

Take a look at your version of what is true
Are these assumptions of God or of you?
Do you create your double bind?
Assuming what isn't a double mind

Then an issue is all it takes for the two to fight
An emotional perspective that will lessen your plight
Shifting gears though will not end the pain
Understanding God and what He says make it easier to contain

Fine for you to say with your words
I feel I am drowning from all your words
I desire attention and comfort, please provide
Who doesn't want these with them and abide?

Can you explain how God, who is all love,
Can give comfort, when He is spirit there above?

Cynicism will gain little, but in complaint
In your desperation you will faint
You understand what I have said
You understand from what you have said

You know from your pondering, what I said is true
It hurts, the truth, not because of offense, but of you

Painful choices of mental or physical degree
Many times due to deprivation with thee
Sin claims to provide a solution as I have said
But using them, you will wind up dead

If the pain is temporary, as God wrote in the Bible
To say He is wrong is outright liable
Follow what He has said and you shall find
How God's ways are compassionate and kind

Forgive, I pray, my complaint that I say
Denying His reality I find I pay
Peace at any price destroys the creation within
I really want to keep it; my hopes on God do I pin.

Session Thirteen

Thank you for your effort and earnestness
It will prevent a much bigger mess
You desire deliverance by God of all
Remember the assumptions and the ball

What would it look like if it came to you?
Would you act on it, what would you do?
Or would you reject it saying it isn't right
I do not see it delivering me from this plight

If that is your choice that you take
As by default, an error then you make
Because your deliverance doesn't match His
The end result, His deliverance you will miss

In your desire to escape the pain
The pain that leaves will come again
The pain that changes tones and color
Changes shape and strength and pallor

The things that make the pain go away
Are feelings of security and validation, wanted now today
You seek comfort and love
The value that fits warm and snug like a glove

You desire release of rejections and isolation's pain
Release from the loss of value, loss of gain
To be listened to when the options are zero
The paths go from wide, to closed, not even narrow

It is trite to count the blessings that you see
Leave the curses; let them be
Count what assets, those of you
We note liabilities; that is true

Broken dreams of crystal glass
The painful bloody mass, alas

Picking up those pieces will only cut you up again
Create anew, lest the work be in vain
Recreate, but not compromise the future
The bloody hands, washed, sewed with suture

They will work again, on dreams anew
Pray to God to do His will; a surprise is then awaiting you
You may grieve the loss then let it go
This you must do, or you won't grow

Understand what is and what is not in reality
We know then what is and what is not me
We can see the feelings of guilt and shame
We see which are their portions and their blame

Understand the speed of your recovery
Ignorance and knowledge, progress and expectancy
Energy and why of motivation
What must I change to rebuild my elation?

I sense you've said this stuff before
Must you say it many times, and many more?

I want to assure you it is right
To be wrong will only make you more uptight
Put what I have said together
When you do, it is quite a storm that you can weather

Step back, time and again
You will see better than back then
Step back once more; you see your mind and its motives
Step back again; you see your neighbor, your fellow natives

Step back again; you see the world in which you all dwell
Step back again; you see God, and the world that works so
well
Use the lens by which He sees the creation
You will see such sorrow and joyful elation

Beware the claim, a denial of His words divinely said
It is in Hell where they'll make their bed
But see the picture, the whole and your impact
See how you were meant to interact

See your choice, and their choice, to obey or not
Those who do, and those who don't, and what they've got
How and what this means of values and values that are true
We can see illusion and reality, others and what is God's due

Do what He requires, before your body is committed to the fire
This may not stop the pain, but it grants a peace that will never tire

After all is said and done
We have to begin as we begun
The pain remains as I related
But it seems you've only had it rated

You give me reason for hope to seek
Mighty high-sounding words you speak
When events and words trigger powerful emotions
Pushing buttons that demand a sinful promotion

Feelings well up that I cannot stop
No way to end it or the buds to chop
Restrain and see the desires straining there
Demanding release, glaring from their lair

They will turn on me and eat me up
So I try to stop them, as I gulp
These things do not end the pain I feel
They want me to take the bait, then I'll be their meal

Let me put it this way before you go
You think that God doesn't know?
You have faith in Him, which shows in your action
Do you really believe you'll get a negative reaction?

Give Him time and faithful be
Won't you come, feel better, you'll agree
By doing what is important and as you pray
He will open to you every day

Will the pain go away?
Some depends on you, come what may
Responsibility and choices
Working, humility, rejoices

In some ways, that is what it means to bear the cross
Even if the pain isn't one, like your loss
Living in this world is bound to cause a pain
It is caused by sinful desires that we restrain

We hold them back from their action
We hold the thoughts at bay, change our imagination
We change the habits, as we must
We change them because of whom we trust

Perspectives faithful to His will, His call
Work believing God's control in all
As I said, you think God doesn't know?
You doubt this; you can't grow

Assuredly God is faithful to His purpose
Pain or pleasure, rich or poor, better or worse
A marriage vow to life with the Lord
Eyes to see, a heart to love, devotion we can afford

A comfort I would give to thee
A comfort with these words you will see
You are tormented with the wicked, there is no rest
You felt pained, what is my crime, I did my best

The peace you long for is a soul at peace within
The peace you long for is a soul cleansed of sin
It is possible to be tormented by the sin of another
What happened was wrong, actions, or friends' words, or
other

It is their refusal and rejection of you in this case
It is not you, but rejection of a righteous base
You feel the pain that sin does inflict
It feels like torments; I predict

Pain isn't God's rejection of you
Pleasure isn't necessarily God's acceptance too
Blessing and pain come and go
It is his word by it our work we know

It isn't that we are pure in our work or play
It is that we really want to do things God's way
Even if we fail in our effort
People will help, and understand, and support

The peace you long for, and it is yours
In knowing God knows and your hope soars
Not that you will merit more in heaven
But the difference is in the faith you have striven

In keeping the path as well as you can
God will grant the peace to any woman or man
The faithful keeping to the truth He said
Will grant the peace, the solace in work or bed

Peace God knows is in the control, despite distress
My future is assured, despite the loss, trouble, or mess
Peace eyes to see myself, His creature here to bless
This peace passes understanding, grounded in Truth we
profess

Yours the peace that God grants to thee
This is from His salvation for you and me
This peace given to tormented souls within
Tormented who work to do right, not create sin

Living according to His truth He said
Doing His will as best you can, you will be fed
This peace will come, is not being complacent or self-
satisfied
It is not forgiveness, self-bestowed, giving way to pride

Peace comes from God according to His truth
Self praise and gratification comes from a religious market booth
Peace that God grants, to the faithful in word and deed
Peace that God grants is a by-product of faith, and willing to bleed

Peace that God grants will come by overcoming ourselves within
Peace that God grants, we knowing we are not what we have been
God's in control, regardless of what we see
When we're done, we shall, reassured, rest in Thee

You say, "Entrust my soul to God"
Who handles both the blessing and the rod
God will provide without my sight
God will provide strength to fight

When the battles' losses mount
Fight on it is on God that I count
When I've failed the test
Try again, sword in hand and do my best

This is my God to trust
Though Satan buries me in wrongful lust
This is my God, His will to do
Do my part for Him, come through

His is the outcome, His the field
So I will to His Truth yield
This is my God, His Truth shall stand
Even if I am struck down by His hand

This is my God to Him my soul, I entrust
He is a God of love as well as just
The Lord knows the pains I have got
Which are true and which are not

For all the burning I go through
Help me Lord to burn for you
Help me Lord the words to keep
The ones you wrote until I sleep

Help me Lord for me to keep my word
For you are my Creator and my Lord
You are my Creator and Savior
May I honor you with my behavior?

This is my God, I'll bow the knee
When He in glory comes for me
This is my God resigned to His will my Sovereign
May I dear Lord, then, serve you in heaven?

Session Fourteen

The road is long, the walk in day and night
Will you walk with me as walk in His light?
Helping each other when we fall
Knowing the Lord will help, The Lord of all

Tis hard to trust when one is in pain
The fight is on two fronts, nay three, I dain
Fight one is doing what is right
Doing right despite the inward painful plight

A mind that offers choices of divided loyalties
To train the mind, to take the godly, not the hostilities
To be sure the actions taken are ones that the Lord will bless
Choose the right, not compromise or digress

The second fight is the fight of the senses
To discipline the body to obey though it tenses
It will do what you will
Not the things for pain or thrill

The third fight that is fought
Not the mind or body or frame of thought
It is the faith in which I have my being
It is the faith that knows without seeing

It is the faith that fights on day to day
It fights to do, to God I'll pray

Even in His silence, I believe He knows
God grant me faith, that is strength that grows
Help me Lord to live up to these words I say
Lest I fall and forget, if I do I'll ever pay

Help me to be true to these words I utter
In time of decision, my heart will flutter
Grant that I may not shrink from the choice that is right
Grant that it might be true in your sight

This choice is not by my wisdom, or reason
But guided by your word, the salted season
It is faith that knows my God and Lord
A faithful creator that severs the silver cord

Lord grant that I may ever serve on bended knee
In life, in death, may my soul be stayed on thee
Remember me in your kingdom one once said
When you were hanging in agony and blood red

Grant I may faithful be, in my cross I take for thee
The day to day, my struggle to walk, remember me
You Sir, would walk with one as me?
A poor choice, can't you see?

I see the faith that wants to work on the Lord's side
I want to be one with such a conviction, with them abide

I am not healed, as you know
I still have many days, to work through this woe
Though others have troubles of their own
Why choose me, when I moan?

I see faith you cannot see
It is a faith I want for me
The way to learn from this walk
Is to walk, and learn from our talk

I am a painful stranger for your company
If that is what you want to see
I will still desire to be true God
I until the soul is to the Lord, body beneath the sod

I will work as I can under heaven's dome
Then in death, I will behold the lights of home

A comfort I would give to thee
A comfort with these words you will see
You are tormented with the wicked, there is no rest
You feel pained, what is my crime, I did my best

The peace you long for is a soul at peace within
The peace you long for is a soul cleansed of sin
It is possible to be tormented by the sin of another
What happened was wrong, words to warn sister, brother

Their refusal and rejection of you in this case
It is not you, but rejection of a righteous base
You feel the pain that sin does inflict
If feels like torment I predict

The peace you long for, and it is yours
Is knowing God knows, and your hope soars
Not that you merit more in heaven
But the difference is the faith that you have striven

In keeping the path as well as you can
God will grant the peace to any woman or man
The faithful keeping to the truths as He said
Will grant the peace, the solace, at work or bed

Peace, God knows and is in control despite distress
My future is assured, despite the trouble or the mess
Peace, eyes to see myself, as His creature here to bless
Peace passes understanding grounded in the truth that we
profess

Yours, the peace that God grants to thee
This is from His salvation for you and me
This peace given to tormented souls within
Tormented who work to do right not to create sin

Living according to His truth, He said
Doing His will, as best you can, you will be fed
This peace will come is not self-complacency
It is not self-bestowed forgiveness that is spiritual indecency

Peace comes from God according to His truth
Self-praise and gratification come from a religious market
booth
Peace that God grants to the faithful in word and deed
Peace that God grants, a by-product of work and willingness
to bleed

Peace that God grants will come by overcoming can'ts
Peace that God grants by doing right and all our sin recants

Things that torment the mind, burning bridges
Things that divide the mind, forcing wedges
The unending dull groaning
The anguish of the moaning

It is a number of things
Their facts and reason, its false truth rings
Self-doubt in the midst of thee
To doubt the faith of God on bended knee

It claims doubt, the comfort in the midst of pain
Where is the promise, His peace doesn't reign
Pain that you feel is not doubt
Comfort delayed is not what faith is all about

Where is the peace I have heard so much?
It is a peace I cannot touch
It comes and goes like a tide
Accept its fickleness I can't abide

Is it the peace or your faith that is fickle?
By our attitudes, our notions, it can be a flood or a trickle
You know who God is and that He does care
Let God be God, earth be earth, and air be air

Let others be as they see fit
God is in your knowledge of all for ill or benefit
I am sorry for the pain you feel
It runs deep, still to God make your appeal

Continue as you can, as you will and work
Faith in God's answer as His child is your perk
God will answer that is sure
Let us watch and wait and endure

God will answer yes, no, wait, or other
In ways unknown like child to father or mother

This is the trust we have, come what may
Come pain or threats from one or they

Our lot to live and learn His will
When we have learned it drill, drill, drill
Not because we do not know
It is by this that we will grow

When the battle shout is given
It will show for what we're striven
Those who know will surely survive
At battle's end, you'll be alive

That is well and good I guess
How long the healing, how long the mess

God will grant the answers to the prayers
But it is according to His will, not our cares
It is still granting of what is right
It will still put all wrong and ill to flight

Trust in truth the God we cannot see
He will rescue thee
When you do as He said
Then peace will come as you read

I feel beyond the reach of anybody
If they care they can't touch me
The pit of depression is longer than their rope
This is, I feel, a reason that puts me beyond hope

Should it happen that there is care, by even one
I haven't the strength to hang on, I come undone

You've been doing what God says, I trust

Yes, I have, but the pains remain, my faith to rust

Regardless of what you may see
Faith is restless, until Christ is in thee

Examine the pains, what can they do?
Nothing, nor can they corrode you
This gives rise to conviction
In our lives from opening prayer to benediction

You come faithfully and spoke of "hardship"
I will relate to you, I have seen in you the sonship
By this you carry on from morning to night
Cheerful, to many, who are unaware of your fight

You carry on not making excuses
Those who do have many ruses
You try to do what you can as you can
Thus by your effort show yourself a man

This is the faith that the Bible people used
They were persecuted and abused
You have now this growing faith of old
You will, by this, grow more bold

You have the faith and love and hope to die
When the time comes to heaven, you'll fly
I thank you for your example it keeps me on track and not to
roam
Then I am sure your faithful eyes will see the lights of home

Yet I feel hollow, never to be filled
I feel threatened, always never to be stilled
I feel the cold, a relationship now forbidden
I feel the answer lies, truth forever hidden

I feel no relief, though I press for a solution
I feel I may never get the absolution
I feel no refuge from this storm
Being alone in a fight like this becomes the norm

I feel useless, what help am I?
I feel bound for the place of endless fry
A still small voice in the night
A voice to relieve the despair and the fright

Though your pain may last 100 years
Though your pain brings a flood of tears
Though the flames burn but not consume
Though your life feels doom and gloom

It is hard to live when another oppresses you
It is harder still when it is unjust through and through
The weight increases when Satan adds his finger
The pain, never really goes away, all it does is linger

The weight that you have bore
Satan will try to get you to think it's more
Life as incidental as you live with pains and hurt
Can hinder spiritual sight or make you more alert

Advice is easy when one doesn't bear the loads
It is hard to apply when Satan with temptation goads
Prove the serpent wrong in the faithfulness of Job
It is war, guard God's value, and what to God is owed

Stand guard, though Satan doesn't play fair
He will cheat, trip you up and be ever there
The pressures on those who try to remain pure
In the end God will indeed bring resurrection cure

Your life will bring a charge, yea, counter, charge, on the foe
(Satan)
Your life is evidence for God's prosecution, don't you know?
Here is the one, you (Satan) sought to cause me to frown
It is God's victory, but Satan will be cast down

But there is no help to the pain I must say
It does not end and continues day to day

Faith that as you carry on and do as you must
You will continue, God knows and delivers on those who trust
You have a choice on those things you sense
Freedom to act or build a fence

Being aware of the sin is not a crime (sin)
Desire alone is not spiritual grime (sin)

Pain, caused by another, you are deprived
You then suffer, does not mean sin has arrived
To suffer from life's inequalities, do not be bitter
By handling it right, makes us more for heaven fitter

For a brief moment in time I had a minute of peace
A drop of the sublime, I had a tiny piece
What world is this where there is bird song
The sun is warm; the conflict was long

The clouds of depression are leaving
Their heaviness, a weight is lifted, no more heaving
I can stand not bowed 'neath a load
No longer is a muddy cave my adobe

My sword is nicked in 1,000 places
It is still sharp to their aces
The ground is as barren as the moon
It was still dark though it is noon

Now the blue, is that the sky?
Been so long I could cry
But tears were spent long ago
Been so long I've forgotten, now I know

Marching home, orders now are given
What is that hymn they are sing'n?
I looked at the enemy line
It looked so strong and ever fine

Their wall collapsed this dawn, I've seen
What it revealed turned us green
We fought long and hard to hold the line
Commander's order charge, victory by his design

I asked him how, and gave him the glory
Don't my son, and said another story
God's the one to give the praise
He is the one, The Ancient of Days

The call to watch and arms again
The enemy re-assembled as they had been
The sky clouded up as before
I thought, oh no, more blood and gore

This time will not be so long now
I thought, you have fought you know how
You now have greater faith beyond the cloud
You faith will carry you as you vowed

The dream ended with a battle fighting they renew
Depressing I thought, but I've a word from home, it's true
The dream ends in a fight, adrenaline flowing
Once again my mind dizzy, grapples for knowing

Despair in the future, yet with hope fight on
Using what I've got, though it still weighs a ton

Many things in life are incidental
Our bodies, how smart or mental
Our income that we have and family
These things beyond our choice for you and me

Life events of death and accident
Disaster, sickness, errors, not what we meant
They happen but make no difference to the King of Kings
What makes a difference in our lives is how truth rings

Things of this world will surely go away
It's our character to God and to what He said, come what may
What is your confidence in?
Anything but God would be a sin

I understand you want security, comfort, and to be warm
I understand you tire of depression and its fear, alarm
Security is what you will get, be assured
Your cup will overflow, unmeasured

The choices are yours this day
Heed the Lord and what He does say

Feelings come and go, this we know
Your choice as to what can hinder or make you grow
Feelings of others can cause us to feel sad
That is their problem so do not be mad

What you say is well and good and most kind
But my sight is twisted, my eyes are blind
My self-image is twisted, I cannot see me
I cannot see you clearly, nor the advice from thee

Self-image lost in the loss of being married
Too little too late, the help it tarried
My ability to provide for my family hurts, a stain
I seem unable to do better; I guess I am to blame

The divorce threatened and destroyed much of it
Now it is lost, nothing to build, I have not the grit

You have faith in God, and God in you
You have love for God, and God loves you

You have hope in God and God's hope for you
A relationship, you the salt, a recipe careful how you stew
Remember these things, the noble things on which to think
Remember the river of living water, and you may have a drink

We will walk and talk and pray
Things get hard and fight, the spirit's fray
To forgive, and not bear that anger's weight
Let God be just, it will help to enter in God's gate

God will heal, do His will, and He will with you abide
God will bless, and to heaven an angel will be our guide

Oh the waves of depression swell
They can drown the mind where it does dwell

The battles rage from time to time to time
An unending battle I am thrust into, what a crime
I will try to do what you have said
Understand, I need aid for I have bled

It goes on and on, the pain in the gut
A circle, I think, O.K., then I am not O.K., then, but
I feel starved to be somebody, a trove
I feel starved to be loved and to love

I feel starved for me to pursue my dreams
Afraid, lest one tear at the seams
I cannot bear rebellion or non-compliance
Being stonewalled, I feel no self-reliance

Yet it is they, or one, that I must talk to
I cannot find another way through

There are no heroics, in self-shame
There are no heroics, in self-blame

I know there is nothing in such feelings
I know emotions as those, there are no healings
I am not talking about sin, as God said, "No" therein
Where is the nourishment from without and from within?

What is sanctioned by God and what is not?
Hard to maintain feelings and untie the knot
I feel abandonment, and some ask, where is your joy?
I am too mournful, to people, it is a pity poy

It is hard to battle beside the lust
The bitterness, anger and loss of trust

I will be with you when the battle swells
I will be with you for water from dry wells
I will help you when you have lost your hope
I will help you when faith you reach for and grope

You have given me help in seeing your conviction
To carry on even when you see life's contradiction

These things may never see an end, you realize
Never until we travel to the skies

I understand the cycles of life's battles and the war

Though crippled, I know God and what I'm fighting for
I want to say to God, "I fought the good fight," says I
The providence of God, that grace, that faith, is, Why I Want to Die.

End

Parting Reflections

Patient's Prayer

Lord, please hark to my plea
I make this on bended knee
Have mercy on me I pray
Grant I may have a new marriage day

This pain within is hard for me to take
A hand chosen one lest I make another mistake
Lord, please answer my plea
Have mercy on your servant, me

Send me word that it is O.K.
Send me word, please I pray
A hope you, Lord, will have mercy on me
That is why I lift this prayer to thee

I know your compassion, I have read
You even raised people who were dead
I know you will answer in times like this
When one is down and in deep distress

I cannot rely on what I want and feel alone
It is your word, which grants healing and for sin atone
Again, I ask and make a plea
Would you grant a chosen wife for me?

Suited for each other's wants and needs
May we help you spread your seed?
Grant I may listen well
I don't want to go to Hell

Please answer, so I will understand
I want to get to the Promised Land
Thank you, Lord, for answer of the plea
I know you will answer and come for me

The load becomes greater than I can bear
Help me please; you say you care
Options lost and feeling humiliation
I feel an eternal condemnation

There is no peace with daily throbbing pain
In living life I feel no gain
Even happy goals that people set before me
Fail to enthrall, cause hope, they only annoy, let me be

My battle is not over, it rages still
Emotions fight wisdom's will
There are those who add to the pain as well
They say if I marry, I shall go to Hell

What does the text say, is it really that unclear?
Both sides say that, "Truth resides with me here"
What would Jesus have said, I wonder, to those in such a mess?
What would He say, what would Jesus confess?

If things were as that, decided over the marriage and one's
salvation
Surely Jesus would have made this clear, to show one's devotion
The therapist cannot help much in this regard
The convictions must be mine, but to get it is hard

The growing sense if I cannot remarry, then I will die
The emotions growing, I will not care the why
Lord, grant me strength to find your intent, your will
Context of words, language, the message, what skill

The sad truth is that I may have to walk alone now
Grant that she will come, we will walk together if God's will allow
To walk away from those who claim I am wrong as wrong as can
be
The devil works to divide and all in the name of purity

The devil divides in the name of a compromised compassion
So sin can live and ignore the God's true lesson
Lord, keep me in thy truth and salvation
I want to make it to heaven

It will come by your grace, that is sure
But only, by your faith I endure
This is hard to walk, torn asunder by competing doctrines of
heaven
Which is right, to discern the way to walk the bread, the leaven

My own conscience it seems will now ever bleed
Relationships torn, and others who cannot succeed
The God who helps those who failed, and failed again
How to help, to mend the heart, the struggling man's bane

The purity in heart and doctrine are important, this is true
But at what expense, to alienate the sinner, you?
To err is human, in sin and carrying out God's will
Lord, grant me wisdom, to stand in love and truth, a bitter pill

Lord, grant this servant mercy, as I carry out your saving grace
Truth, I do, in love, mistakes, forgive me, and may I see your face?

A parting poem:

I hope not to mind to walk alone I guess.
With God at hand, He will bless
Grant eyes to see and the relationships recognize
Not only emotion, but providence, your word will finalize

AMEN

The convictions hard won, what I now have believed
Born from pain, Lord, grant I am not deceived
The final outcome from study I have done
The weights of condemnation weighed a ton

The muscles sore and mind from mental strain
I try to live in purity, but Lord cleanse us from sin's stain
The word is given I may be given a wife
The request is granted, maintain your life

I was in shock, my strength left, I sat down
I am granted my heart's desire, to God I am bow'n
New strength came, a vitality I did not have before
New strength to carry on the fight, as faith's lore

Lord, thank you for this gift of hope in your will
May I uphold her, in better, for worse, health and ill
For richer, poorer, grant us strength to live for you
It is by your strength and word that will get us through

This final chapter of verse draws to a close
Help us to do thy will, what you chose
The days ahead, happy with you, we hope, and content
May we follow the straight path and not the bent

Thank you, Lord, on bended knee
Thank you, Lord, for my wife in humility
Help us, Lord, to do what you have said
Help us to do what, as your Bible, we have read

Our faith in your character and providential care
Guide us to the heaven's gate, may you greet us there
Help us to help each other in doing what you say
Help us to do your will, starting on bended knee each day

To God be the glory, in Jesus's name we pray.